EARLY MODERN EUROPEAN CIVILIZATION AND ITS POLITICAL AND CULTURAL DYNAMISM

THE MENAHAM STERN JERUSALEM LECTURES

Sponsored by the Historical Society of Israel and published for
Brandeis University by University Press of New England

Series Editors:
Yosef Kaplan, senior editor, Department of the History of the Jewish
  People, The Hebrew University of Jerusalem, former chairman of
  the Historical Society of Israel
Michael Heyd, Department of History, The Hebrew University of
  Jerusalem, former Chairman of the Historical Society of Israel
Shulamit Shahar, professor emeritus, Department of History, Tel-Aviv
  University, member of the Board of Directors of the Historical Society
  of Israel

For a complete list of books in this series, please visit www.upne.com
and www.upne.com/series/MSL.html

Heinz Schilling, *Early Modern European Civilization and Its Political and
Cultural Dynamism*

Brian Stock, *Ethics through Literature: Ascetic and Aesthetic Reading in
Western Culture*

Fergus Millar, *The Roman Republic in Political Thought*

Peter Brown, *Poverty and Leadership in the Later Roman Empire*

Anthony D. Smith, *The Nation in History: Historiographical Debates
about Ethnicity and Nationalism*

Carlo Ginzburg, *History, Rhetoric, and Proof*

EARLY MODERN EUROPEAN CIVILIZATION AND ITS POLITICAL AND CULTURAL DYNAMISM

Heinz Schilling

THE MENAHEM STERN JERUSALEM LECTURES

Brandeis
University
Press

Historical
Society of
Israel

PUBLISHED BY UNIVERSITY PRESS OF NEW ENGLAND

Hanover and London

88558580580657005806570046580657004658065700465806570046

Brandeis University Press/Historical Society of Israel
Published by University Press of New England,
One Court Street, Lebanon, NH 03766
www.upne.com

Library of Congress Cataloging-in-Publication Data

Schilling, Heinz.
Early modern European civilization and its political and cultural
dynamism / Heinz Schilling.
    p.   cm. — (The Menaham Stern Jerusalem lectures)
Includes bibliographical references and index.
ISBN-13: 978–1–58465–700–2 (cloth : alk. paper)
ISBN-10: 1–58465–700–6 (cloth : alk. paper)
1. Europe—History—1492–1648. 2. Reformation. 3. Counter-
Reformation. 4. Religious refugees—Europe—History—16th century.
5. Religious refugees—Europe—History—17th century. 6. Social
change—Europe—History—16th century. 7. Social change—Europe—
History—17th century. 8. Europe—Historiography. I. Title.
D228.S36   2008
940.2'3—dc22   2007049126

Contents

v

Contents

Foreword

The Jerusalem Lectures in History given in Memory of Menahem Stern in the year 2006 were given on May 8, 9, and 11 by Prof. Heinz Schilling. Since 1992, Prof. Schilling has held the Chair for the History of the Early Modern Period at the Humboldt-Universität of Berlin. Before that he was Professor at the universities of Gießen and Osnabrück, and Assistant Professor and Lecturer in Bielefeld. He studied history, German language and literature, philosophy, and sociology at Cologne and Freiburg im Breisgau, and received his PhD in History in 1971 from the University of Freiburg.

Heinz Schilling possesses an unusually broad international background. He has been Visiting Member at the Institute for Research in the Humanities of the University of Wisconsin, Madison, and at the Center for Western European Studies of the University of California, Berkeley, as well as Fellow of the Netherlands Institute for Advanced Study. He is a member, since 2005, of the Academia Europæa. In Germany, he spent the academic year 2004/5 as Fellow of the Historisches Kolleg in Munich, where I had the pleasure of making his personal acquaintance.

Prof. Schilling has had a full share of academic tasks and honors. Shortly after arriving as Professor at the Humboldt-Universität of Berlin in 1992, he was called to serve as the founding dean of its re-established Faculty of Humanities.

He acts, since 1994, as European Managing Editor of the "Archive for Reformation History" and since 2001 as Chair of the Society for Reformation History. He is Member of the scientific board of the Deutsches Historisches Museum of Berlin, Member of the Berlin-Brandenburgische Akademie der Wissenschaften, Corresponding Member of the British Academy, and Foreign Member of the Koninklijke Nederlandse Academie van Wetenschappen. The latter acknowledged Prof. Schilling's achievements by bestowing upon him, in 2002, the Dr. A. H. Heineken-Prize for Historical Sciences.

Prof. Schilling's scientific oeuvre is exceptionally broad and variegated. He is the author of eleven scientific books, in German, Italian, and English. Of the latter, mention should be made of *Civic Calvinism in Northwestern Germany and the Netherlands, Sixteenth to Nineteenth Centuries* (1991), and of *Religion, Political Culture, and the Emergence of Early Modern Society: Essays in German and Dutch History* (1992). Prof. Schilling has edited or co-edited nineteen volumes of collective studies, and presented, in two volumes, an important source collection, *Die Kirchenratsprotokolle der reformierten Gemeinde Emden, 1557–1620* (1989, 1992). As of early August 2007, he has published a staggering 158 scientific articles, mostly in German but also in Dutch, French, Italian, Spanish, and English, in such leading journals as *Histoire sociale* (Social history), *The Sixteenth Century Journal, Journal of European Modern History*, as well as in the *International Encyclopedia of the Social and Behavior Sciences* (2001). Not content with academic venues, he counsels and organizes historical exhibitions, initiates and appears on radio and television programs on historical topics, and writes in the daily press.

Prof. Schilling sees his main areas of work in the compar-

ative history of Europe in the Early Modern period; towns
and town burghers from the Late Middle Ages to the early
nineteenth century; migration and minorities in pre-modern
Europe; the social history of northwestern European Calvinism and its mentality; the history of the Reformation
and Confessionalization; and the history of political theory
and international relations in the sixteenth and seventeenth
centuries, topics that are treated extensively in the present
volume.

In an ongoing process of dialogue with previous tendencies in German and international historiography, Prof.
Schilling is reintroducing religion as a key factor in interpretation of the early modern period, and especially for understanding its specific way of social change. In his work and
in this book, he is charting the intricate ways in which a
previously unified Latin Christianity was able to modernize
by differentiating into nations, states, and confessional religions. Modernity, in the view he systematically develops in
this volume, was then not about getting rid of religion, but
about allocating it new functions, a new modus operandi,
and a new place in the web of institutions making up Early
Modern Europe.

—Michael Toch
The Hebrew University
of Jerusalem

I Introduction: The History of Europe between National and Global Challenge

This work has given me an invaluable opportunity to reappraise my ideas on the key structures and mechanisms that enabled Europe to embark on processes of fundamental change from medieval to early modern and modern forms in society, politics, and culture. To look upon Europe and its history from the southeast across the Mediterranean Sea offers a new perspective on early modern European history, a perspective that is both distant and close. Just so were the Jews, from earliest times on, both entwined with yet apart from European history.

In consequence of a long tradition that focused on princes, their courts and territories, and later on national states, historiography has been organized in Europe along a national framework, in research, in school and university teaching, and in public discussions. However, because during the early modern period "Europe" became the dominant category of transterritorial and transnational self-understanding,[1] there existed a complementary historiographical tradition concerned with the history, identity, and common culture of European societies and their civilization as a whole. Marc Bloch's famous and often quoted article published in 1928 "Pour une histoire comparée des sociétés européennes"[2] gave this branch of the European historiographical tradition a theoretical basis that after the Second World War empowered historians to surmount the boundaries of national historiography, especially through the instrument of comparison.[3] This European perspective in history was enormously strengthened by the political process of European unification, which resulted in a common market, a common currency, and coordinated defense, foreign, and education policies. Especially during the last decade of the twentieth century, when the European Union and the introduction of the euro produced a wave of Europe enthusiasm, several multivolume histories of Europe went into press.[4] At the same time the European Science Foundation (ESF) at Strasbourg as well as some national scholarly councils started impressive research programs in comparative European history or—as in the National Science Organization (NWO) of the Netherlands—programs for national history "in European perspective."[5] The same refocusing held true for theoretical and systematic questions of cultural transfer, institutional settings, or the organization of political power.[6]

In spite of these and similarly impressive efforts to overcome the traditional national perspectives in European historiography, these sprouts of a transnational historical culture of Europe are at present in danger of being swept away by two new historiographical waves, the one emphatically retrogressive, the other emphatically progressive. The retrogressive wave is the consequence of two crises. First, crisis within the European Union caused by the failure of the European Constitution and the consequent rise of new nationalisms, especially within the new European Union members (Poland among others). Second, the crisis of the concept of multicultural societies on the other hand, with the resulting pressure for the integration of migrants along clear lines of traditional national identities. Recent immigrant riots, fundamentalist bombings, and assassinations have produced

4

shock waves, resulting in grassroots demands not only for basic security and stability, but also for a clear rejection of cultural relativism. For historians this latter demand means, first and foremost, a renaissance of discussions on national identity; it calls for the creation of a canon for the learning and interpretation of respective national histories (a movement that is especially strong in the Netherlands, the former El Dorado of multiculturalism and postnationalism).[7] Politicians and intellectuals alike have became aware that, at least for the moment, when it comes to organizing and guaranteeing welfare, social and legal security, or physical protection against attacks by terrorists, there does not exist a real alternative concept or institutional framework to the national state and its national society. Consequently, national categories also enjoy at present a renaissance with regard to political programs for the future as well as for historical analysis or synthesis.[8]

Parallel to this nationalist challenge the concept of European history has been undermined by a second historiographical wave, one that was also launched by real developments in politics and economy: the process of globalization, a process that has accelerated quite swiftly in the past few years. Ironically, at the very time that Europe was preparing to introduce the euro, Europe itself was waning as the central concern for politicians, economists—and tourist managers—as well as for scientists and scholars. Their most fascinating objective today is the entire globe. Whereas scientists and also social scientists concerned with present-day societies and world affairs could cope easily with the new, enlarged framework, it is not so easy for historians working on periods before 1800 to find an adequate response to the historiographical challenge of globalization. Intellectually, they are inhabitants of a "World we have lost,"[9] and

that world was not at all shaped by an experience comparable with that of present-day globalization. Nevertheless, it
is quite clear that historians cannot simply go on with their
national state–type history in the manner of the nineteenth
century. Neither can they postpone their response to globalization's challenge to some future time *after* they have
finished the integration of these national histories into an
overarching European history. Indeed, there are already fascinating experiments with global history, among which are
two of specific interest to historians of early modern Europe.
In his book entitled *1688* the American historian John Wills
gives a *tour d'horizon* of the world of great commercial com-
panies and the logistics of wooden ships, of courts and resi-
dences, of world religions and their counterparts, and—last
but not least—of the anthropological dimension of exile,
hope, and family.[10] And Herman van der Wee, the distinguished Belgian economic historian, in a brilliant essay on
techniques of commerce and financing uncovers the roots
of globalization in the medieval and early modern European
industrial and commercial centers of Bruges, Antwerp, Amsterdam, and London, whose merchants and entrepreneurs
conquered the markets of Asia, Africa, and America by constructing networks all around the globe.[11]

Historians of European history can ignore neither the national nor the global challenge. But their response must be
commensurate with the profile of European civilization and
its history. The diversification by regions, states, and nations
is unquestionably a central and integrative part of European
civilization; consequently, it merits consideration in every
synthesis in European history, at least for the epochs from
the late Middle Ages to the end of the twentieth century.[12]
And, as present-day globalization is, after all, the product
of late medieval and early modern European expansion, in-

evitably every history of Europe has to include a certain amount of world affairs. But of course, the modern type of "global history" under consideration here means more than this traditional truism of early modern and modern Europe's involvement in the history of other world civilizations and, in the end, even more than its forerunner or overview type of global history such as those of Wills and van der Wee. It means a methodological and theoretical challenge that, in my opinion, historians of Europe can best meet by adopting a comparative approach similar to that of Shmuel Eisenstadt's comparative work in world sociology. The historian, who has traditionally treated periods as shaped by regional rather than global experience, and who in addition has been bound to sources and cultural contexts more strictly than has the social scientist, can respond best to the challenge of globalization by adopting comparative approaches.

In my understanding, historians working on the early periods before 1800, which were characterized by exclusively or predominately regional and local experience, can contribute to global history best by constructing and comparing *types of world civilizations.*[13] From this perspective it would be the task of historians of medieval and early modern Europe to elaborate the European type of civilization as an instrument for comparison with other types of world civilization. The aim would be to identify the specific structures and institutions and economic, social, or cultural functions that characterized the respective civilization and distinguished it from others and that opened or closed paths to its internal development or fundamental societal change. This last question, the ability (or inability) of a civilization to generate fundamental social change, is one that any comparison of world civilizations must discuss.

On the whole, such an approach entails a kind of systematic, intellectual arrangement similar to the theoretical experimentalism of the natural sciences. As is self-evident with scientific experiments, such a comparison of world civilizations in the humanities also presupposes (1) clearly defined scientific terms; (2) a clear understanding of the key structures and functions of societies and civilizations; and (3) a rational model of change and its cultural, social, and legal presuppositions. At the same time this scientific approach to history (Geschichtswissenschaften) which incorporates newly developed disciplines—ethnic studies, feminism—into its models and concepts, might offer an adequate response to the accusation of relativism—an accusation increasingly hurled at both history and the humanities (Geisteswissenschaften) in general.[14]

In this approach the European type of civilization has to be identified more precisely as a Latin European type, which differs fundamentally from that of Greek Orthodox Europe. The difference began with the language and meaning of Scripture, as Eastern Christianity was never so successful as the Latin West in establishing absolute uniformity in the language and Scripture of the church.[15] Furthermore, Orthodox Europe must be distinguished from Latin Europe with regard to culture in general: its institutions, functions, and structural framework.[16] In our comparative approach this distinction is purely descriptive and no longer normative or even moral—as was often the case in traditional Central and West European historiography, which constructed a general West-Ost-Gefälle (West to East decline), mainly at the expense of Poland, which in our concept, of course, is part of Latin Europe. In addition, this typological distinction gives access to the borderlands between both civilizations, whose history nearly vanished during the World War and cold war periods of the last century. It also draws attention to various processes of osmosis and diffusion between the two European civilizations rarely discussed by historians in Central or West Europe, but so obvious to travellers through the Baltic republics and Ukraine, where multiconfessionalism has had a great renaissance after the collapse of communist atheism. In particular, the congregations based on the Union of Brest (1595–1596)—by which the Orthodox of Lithuania accepted the Roman doctrines but kept their own liturgical practices and languages as well as their own distinctive customs (for example, married clergy)—were and are part of both Latin and Greek civilizations.[17] Together with this geographical framework a more precise temporal framework is also in order, especially with regard to the above-mentioned question of change. To address the question of why, how, and by which institutions and cultural settings Latin Europe developed the specific and apparently unique dynamism that resulted in fundamental change and ultimately in the transition to modernity, historians must focus on the early modern period from about 1350/1400 to 1750, with special interest in the late sixteenth and early seventeenth centuries. They must pursue a kind of—to adaptat Reinhard Koselleck's terminology of the late eighteenth century—"*Vor-Sattelzeit der Moderne*" (saddling up for modernity).[18]

With regard to the comparative perspective mentioned above, several key features or basic structures can be identified as characteristic of the Latin European type of world civilization[19]: the strong position of "law" and "justice" based on the Roman and canon law tradition; the specific concept and historical manifestation of "Liberty" or "Liberties" rooted respectively in Jewish theology and Greek philosophy; strong communal elements within the political as well as societal and ecclesiastical organisation (the parochial-congregational principle); dualistic reverence between the sacral and the secular, between the ecclesiastical and the civil organization, which, from the very beginning displayed a tendency toward secularization; the strong impact of migration and minorities, especially in its distinct form of "confessional migration" as a result of the Reformation and subsequent formation of early modern confessional churches; the process of state building; and the emergence of an international system based on international law and autonomy and equality of each of its members.

The following chapters discuss in detail those key features that during the sixteenth and seventeenth centuries (accelerating during the decades around 1600, characterized above as an early modern threshold-*Vorsattelzeit* period) became of specific importance for Europe's dynamic capacities; that is, its ability for fundamental change. Chapter 2 deals with the confessionalization of Latin Christianity and its push for religious, political, social, and cultural differentiation of early modern and modern Europe. Chapter 3 treats the closely related confessional migration and the establishment of religious minorities within the Christian host societies—societies that in the long run became leading agents of economic as well as social and cultural change. Chapter 4 deals with the rise of the international state system as a forebear of the Latin European type of civilization. This field is already well researched; my claim here is that Europe gained its decisive dynamism during the decades around 1600 by its close alliance with the process of confessionalization.

Europe's dynamism is based on its confessionalis—

II   The Confessionalization
of European Churches and
Societies—an Engine for
Modernizing and for Social
and Cultural Change

The Religious Profile of Latin Europe

As already touched upon at the outset, the Latin-European type of civilization was characterized by a deep and wide spectrum of relations between religion and society and between church and state with far-reaching consequences not only for the political, social, and cultural profile of a given epoch, but also, and even more influentially, with a decisive impact on the European capacity for fundamental change up to the ultimate breakthrough to modernity in culture, society, state, and their international relations.[1]

Europe, after all, is not simply the result of changes in demography, economics, politics, or affairs of state. The core of Europe has been above all molded by spiritual and cultural processes that for nearly two millennia have been centered on religion.[2] Only at the end of the eighteenth century did secularization gain the upper hand, and even this was largely a rebellious child of religion. Doubtless, to a considerable extent in the late eighteenth and during the nineteenth century modernity had to be installed and defended against clerical restrictions, especially after the Catholic Church, by issuing the syllabus of *Eighty Errors of the Time* (published by Pope Pius IX, December 8, 1864, had revealed itself to be an antimodernist, antiliberal institution. But there can be also no doubt that the capacity of Latin Europe for perpetual change was anchored deeply in its socioreligious profile. The process of fundamental change, which was launched during the sixteenth century at the latest, was established in confrontation to religion; it also, however, generated considerable new dynamics through its debates on religion, ecclesiology, and the principles of the church-state relationship.

The alliance or coalition between religious and political as well as social change was especially powerful and influential during the Reformation and subsequent Confessional epoch from the late fifteenth to the first part of the seventeenth centuries. My hypothesis is that decisive preconditions for Europe's turn onto paths of modernization were installed, not in opposition to the religious forces of confessionalization prevailing in that epoch, but closely intertwined with them, making the confessional epoch in Europe—namely the decades around 1600—to be a "Vorsattelzeit der Moderne" (saddling up for modernity). These dramatic developments of the Reformation and Confessionalization period were only part of a much longer context, which I must outline here by some general remarks.

First, Christian theology never succeeded in monopolizing religion in Europe. Europe has always had a significant Jewish Diaspora, and Islam has also exerted an influence, at least on the eastern and southwestern periphery. In addition, popular religion has always been permeated with traces of pagan belief and of magic in particular. Until modern times, however, it had always been Christianity that had set the tone, and any history of Europe must accordingly pay due attention to the Christian churches and denominations.

Second, concerning the impact of religion, especially on social change, there is a deep, systematic difference between Orthodox Eastern and Latin Western Europe, rooted in theological and ecclesiological differences between the two Christian churches and symbolically represented by the famous event of July 16, 1054, when Cardinal Humbert of Silva Candida, the emissary of Pope Leo IX, during a service at the Hagia Sophia (the revered patriarchal Church of Byzantium) laid a papal bull of excommunication against the Orthodox patriarch Michael Kerullarios upon the altar; the patriarch in retaliation declared the Roman Church to be excommunicated. This schism between the Greek Orthodox and the Western Latin churches, rooted in different preconditions and divergent developments during the early Middle Ages, resulted in fundamental differences in theology, church organization, and in ideas about the interaction of the sacred and the profane and hence about the role of religion within the world and about the church-state relationship. Together with the marked differences in the political and societal structures in the East and the West—with regard to Roman law, participation of the estates, urban or communal self-government, and so forth—these theological and ecclesiastical differences resulted in two distinct, and in many respects opposite types of European civilizations and different paths into modernity or even the capacity for modernizing change. Only the Latin-Christian type of civilization was characterized by a close and permanent interaction of the sacred and the profane in nearly all fields.

Third, because of its complex heritage from Jewish, Roman, Greek, and Germanic traditions, the Latin-Christian type of civilization was characterized by the fact that religion and society (or the church and the secular political order) did not constitute separate sectors, as in the modern world of the nineteenth and twentieth centuries, but rather were structurally interwoven and functionally interactive. The sacral and the secular were intertwined, but without merging into one indissoluble unit. This structure was not a monism, but a *dualism* in which the religious and the secular, Church and State, closely intertwined, but in a way that gave each of them independence in its own sector or area of responsibility. This independence is what distinguishes Latin Europe from monistic societies, like those of Greek or Orthodox Europe, which did not develop the same differentiation of religion and politics, with the consequence that certain paths toward modernity were barred.

Fourth, because of this type of church and state relationship, from the very beginning Latin Europe developed a tendency toward *secularization* and toward spiritual as well as political *autonomy*, or—in the terms of Max Weber—toward rationality and modernity. In this context it is important to note that secularization did not develop exclusively (or, indeed, mainly) as an opposition movement to religion and the churches. Secularization frequently drew its decisive inspiration from the Christian religion and philosophy and was sustained by religious movements. Again and again, a religious dynamic was transported into the secular world, where it gave power and legitimacy to both political and social activities.

Fifth, the interjection of religion into the world produced a great deal of brutal violence and suffering that, in retrospect, led to an oppressive burden of guilt. Today, it goes without saying that any analysis of the impact of Christian religion on modernization and modern Europe must include this darker side and both its facets: the internal and the external. The *internal* includes the prosecution of heretics and other forms of dissent during the Middle Ages, the confessional conflicts, and the religious wars, the prosecution of nonconfessional denominations (namely the anti-Trinitarians) and of deists and freethinkers during the early modern period. The *external* includes the Crusades, the pogroms against Jews, the Reconquista and the *limpieza de sangre* (purity of blood) policy in Spain, and the violent mission in connection with European overseas expansion.

Confessionalization and the Acceleration of Social Change around 1600

The late medieval protests, as personified by John Wyclif and the British Lollards or Jan Hus and the Hussite reform movement in Bohemia, showed how fragile the medieval Catholic Church was when confronted with separatist social or protonational forces. These protests established the structural basis for the premodern dynamism of Latin Europe, which came to an apogee during the sixteenth century (actually, rather at its end) by confessionalization rather than by the Reformation itself. Protestantism started as theological and political opposition within the church itself; having failed in its aim of reforming the church as a whole, however, the internal opposition resulted in the rise of different confessional churches. Each of them reclaimed exclusive, universal truth; in the long run, such splintering could not but end in the overturning of traditional universalism and in the emergence of modern forms and structures. This will be demonstrated in chapter 3 with regard to the long-term consequences of confessional migration.

In terms of church history in a stricter sense, the Reformation and its consequences are usually described primarily as a schism, as secession or separation: *Kirchenspaltung*. But this terminology and its negative assessment of its development is not adequate for our approach, which seeks the specific causes of European dynamism and the precondition of modernization. In this perspective, the *Kirchenspaltung* assumes a positive connotation as theological, cultural, political, and institutional differentiation within the Christian world—from the ecclesiastical monoculture of the Middle Ages to the multiconfessionalism of the early modern period and to the religious and societal pluralism of the modern age. In this perspective, Reformation and confessionalization[3] were processes within a much older, general trend that shaped the European type of civilization from the very beginning. This close coalition of religious and social change, of church and state, of religious and secular culture was decisive for the rise of Latin Europe to world primacy. Yet it also produced, and this must not be denied, tremendous harm, grief, conflicts within families and neighborhoods, violence, and—as the French historian Denis Crouzet[4] has shown so impressively—interior wars of unbelievable cruelty. As will be described in more detail,[5] by the early seventeenth century the culmination of these forces led to the catastrophe of a universal war of states and religion, in which European civilization itself was at stake.

Because of the pertinence of religion to secular matters and to the alliance of church and state, the process of confessionalization had an impact on nearly all aspects of private and public life. This impact was especially felt in societies under the *religio-vinculum-socieatits* maxim,[6] which postulated that there could not be any peace or social cohesion within a given society without a common religion. This postulate launched a fundamental social process of change that included changes in religion and church as well as in politics and society, behavior, outlook, and culture. Therefore confessionalization, which from the last decades of the sixteenth century took hold in virtually all the societies and states of Europe, was far from being a brake on social change; indeed, it was an engine to push it ahead. Seen in long-term perspective, confessionalization was one of the driving elements of that transformative process of the early modern period that pushed the Old European society toward the modernity of universal, pluralistic, liberal, and democratic industrial or postindustrial societies.

First and foremost, the differentiation took place within the church itself: The second half of the sixteenth century gave birth to three or four confessional churches of Europe's modern age: the Lutheran Church, the Calvinist/Reformed Church, the Tridentine Catholic Church, and the Anglican Church as a fourth one, if we count the English state church separately, in that it was Protestant in doctrine, but more "Catholic" in ritual and church organization. Each of these claimed to be universal and the "old" or "evangelical" one; in fact, however, each of them, including Roman Catholicism, were new churches of and within early modern Europe. Together with this differentiation went formation and modernization: In contrast to the theologically, institutionally, and as regards religious personnel, more open medieval church, the modern confessional systems were characterized by an unambiguous definition of their principles of dogma, formulated by an explicit confession or *Confessio*: the *Confessio Augustana* of 1530 and the Book of Concord (*Konkordienbuch*) of 1577 of the Lutheran Church; the *Confessiones Helveticae* of 1536 and 1566 together with similar national confessions, the Confessio Gallica, the Confessio Belgica, and so forth, of the Reformed or Calvinist Churches; the Book of Common Prayer and the 39 Articles of 1549 and 1563 respectively of the Anglican Church; and finally the *Professio fidei Tridentina* of 1564 of the Roman Catholic Church. This dogmatic formation was accompanied by a parallel institutional and bureaucratic formation, by professionalization, based on education and training of the personnel of each confessional church, and last but not least, by the rise of modern institutions and mechanisms of control and discipline: visitations in Catholic and Lutheran Churches, the Presbyterian church discipline of the Calvinists, and, of course, the notorious Inquisition. As a result, Europe around 1600 was differentiated into distinct religious and cultural systems that differed markedly in doctrine, rite, spirituality, and in everyday religious culture.

Second, as each confessional church developed its specific confessional culture,[7] the confessionalization of the late sixteenth century resulted in a cultural diversification that even today everybody traveling through Europe will experience, from the countries influenced by Catholicism with their colorful and luxuriant language of images and architecture, to the Lutheran or Reformed countries with more sober, less sensuous display of pictures and a culture of the word—even in music as is demonstrated by the mostly Lutheran Oratorios. Perhaps the most important consequence of these confessional cultures for the present is the difference between Catholic and Protestant—especially Calvinist—culture in the ability or inability to accept and integrate cultural, intellectual, and social impulses from the non-Christian or even nonreligious parts of the modern world.

Third, we must consider the influence of the modern confessional systems on early modern state formation and the formation of the modern international system of power states during the crisis of the first half of the seventeenth century. This topic will be discussed in chapter 4.

Fourth, closely connected with the emergence of the confessional culture and its impact on early modern state formation was its influence on the rise of political identities and nation building.[8] In almost all the countries of Europe, and among almost all the peoples, the formation of a confessional and cultural-political identity was closely connected in time and content. This connection shaped profoundly, and still shapes, the cultural and political profile of the individual nations of Europe. Four distinct areas of cultural and political identity formation can be distinguished in Europe under the influence of confessionalization: the Tridentine Catholic in southern and southwestern Europe; the Lutheran in the German territories and Scandinavia; the Reformed and Calvinist in parts of Switzerland (and also England); and the mixed and multiconfessional area, particularly in the central regions.

The nearest thing to a closed model of early modern confessional identity is provided by Spain on the Catholic and Sweden on the Protestant side. The strong and undisputed Catholic identity of Spain had two roots: the medieval tradition of self-assertion toward the Muslim Arabs, intellectually as well as militarily, and the demands of a composite monarchy with exceptional geographical dimensions (extending from the Iberian Peninsula to southern and northern Italy as well as the Netherlands and to America and Asia) and consequently with a variety of territories with specific political, economic, social, and cultural institutions and interests. According to the *religio vinculum societatis* maxim of the time, these deeply rooted, in many respects contradictory, differences were only to be bridged by a common belief best guaranteed by the new confessionalized system of Tridentine Catholicism. Consequently the new confessional ideology merged with the much older *limpieza de sangre* concept to make ethnic (purity of blood) and confessional homogeneity two sides of the same cleansing process of the Spanish nation—which, by the way, at that time was yet to be constructed! In the European context, this ideology of a nationalistic confessionalized Catholicism became the basis of Spain's claim for hegemony within the rising international system of power states.

All this resulted in the *autos-da-fé* against heretics, starting in the very last years of Charles V's reign and the new pressure on the *conversos* and the New Christians that launched the Iberian migration movement. This migration, notably, was nearly exclusively of Jews; only very, very few Christian Spaniards migrated out of religious reasons—an indicator of the success of the Catholic confessionalization of the Spanish nation, for which, obviously, Protestantism had lost any attractiveness. Since the end of the sixteenth century, Spanish national identity was characterized by a marked aggressiveness against any form of religious and cultural deviance and against aliens on principle. Moors, Jews, *conversos*, and Protestants were particularly stigmatized in terms of disease as the bearers of the *Pestis Germaniae* (the German plague). Significantly, dictionaries even today define *limpieza de sangre* as "originating from a Christian family," the word "Christian" having been a synonym for "Catholic" ever since the sixteenth century. In contrast to the experience of Central Europe, the late Middle Ages in Spain were not characterized by a quest for personal salvation, but by the effect of the collective will to guarantee the purity of doctrine, and to guard against any whiff of heresy. This very early link between striving for purity of dogma and a national awareness that reacted aggressively makes the Spanish immunity to the Reformation plausible, and explains the identification of national interests with those of confessionalized, modern Catholicism, even into the late modern age of the nineteenth and twentieth centuries.

The "nations" in the center of Europe—the Netherlands, Germany, Switzerland—were not able to create similarly clear and monolithic confessional identities, but developed fragmented or multiconfessional identities. Yet Lutheran Sweden in some respect became the Protestant counterpart to Spain in the Catholic camp. For here, too, identification with the Reformation caused comparatively little friction and soon had no real alternative; the Lutheran confessionalization became a decisive support both for the formation of the early modern state and for the rise of Sweden as a European great power. This coupling was of considerable historical significance; perhaps even more important were its consequences for the collective mentality and national awareness of Sweden, which consistently connected its entry into modern times, and the history of internal and external success that it sparked with the Reformation and Lutheran confessionalization.

The precondition for this development was the traditionally close cultural relations in the area of the Baltic and northeast Germany, which had put the Swedes directly within the sphere of influence of the Wittenberg Reformation. The link between Lutheranism and national Swedish identity was decisively consolidated and ideologized politically somewhat later by the fundamental conflict with the Catholic Vasa line in Poland: When, after the death of King Johan III in 1592, his Catholic son Sigismund (king of Poland since 1587) ascended to the Swedish throne (and ruled until 1604), the Scandinavian kingdom was in danger of becoming re-catholized and annexed to Poland. In response to this situation, Charles of Södermanland, younger brother of the deceased and uncle of the new king, organized a rebellion and, as Johan Sigismund refused to abdicate, forced his nephew to leave the country. When in 1604, Charles was formally declared King Charles IX of Sweden (ruling until 1611), a fundamental political, military, and ideological confrontation erupted between the older, catholic line of the Vasa dynasty in Poland and the younger Swedish branch, which remained protestant. In this constellation it was nearly inevitable that, in strong opposition to the catholic enemy family branch in Poland, the Lutheran confession became the ideological fundament for the legitimacy of the protestant Swedish Vasa dynasty as well as for the cultural and national identity of the Swedish people. From the beginning of the seventeenth century, the Lutheranism of the crown was an essential ingredient of the Swedish fundamental laws—a direct parallel to the situation in Catholic France, where the Catholicism of the crown was part of the fundamental laws, and consequently, the Huguenot leader Henri de Bourbon had to convert to become Henry IV, king of France (1589–1610). In Sweden, for generations, Reformation and nation were almost inseparable, and Lutheranism became the focal point of inner cohesion and self-assertion, as well as outward independence and, consequently, one of the engines of the rise to international supremacy, which was installed during the Thirty Years' War by King Gustavus Adolphus (1610–1632), son of Charles IX, who intervened in the Baltic and in Central Europe as savior of the Reformation and protector of his Lutheran brethren.

During the Thirty Years' War, which Sweden waged more decisively than other countries as a battle for the Reformation, the still largely medieval peasant society underwent a swift economic and political modernization. At the same time it succeeded in leaping into the very front rank of the European great powers. This experience of success was combined with the myth of Gustav Adolf, the hero of the faith, who in the fighting (understood in eschatological terms) was seen as the Protestant figure of light conquering the powers of darkness and the Antichrist. This mixture of real historical-political interests and a religious and confessional sense of mission produced that certainty of identity and missionary ethos that gave Sweden inner stability and an expansionist dynamic abroad until the eighteenth century—and also helped it to overcome the deep crisis the conversion of Queen Christina, the daughter of Gustav Adolf, threatened to bring to state and society in the middle of the seventeenth century.

For large stretches of the nineteenth century Lutheran confession and Swedish national identity were largely inseparable; institutionally, too, the Swedish state and the Lutheran Episcopal Church were closely connected. The consequences are evident even today, politically, institutionally, and above all in collective attitudes and identity. In a secularized form the Lutheran, Reformation ethos still gives Swedish society today the certainty that it is on the right path coupled with a sense of duty that it must "convert" the rest of the world to this path. It is the secularized Lutheran identity that determines the historical political culture and the moral awareness of the Swedish "nation" today. Even the structure of individual personality seems to be shaped by this identity—at any rate in the self-interpretation of leading intellectuals. One need only recall the film director Ingmar Bergman, who locates the Lutheran identity as the source of Sweden's neuroses.

Fifth, the rise of the modern, unified, rationally functioning, and disciplined society had great effect in implementing general rules and norms of marriage and family life, education and training, obedience and duty, moral standards and behavior, the role of men and women in the home and in public, and so forth.[9] The fundamental molding of mentality, thinking, and behavior along a Christian code of morals newly defined in the process of confessionalization is most obvious in the case of church discipline by Calvinist presbyteries, struggling tirelessly against deviation in belief and attitudes; against slackness in the observance of church and religious obligations; against dishonesty, violence, and conflict within the congregation and the community; against immodesty, opulence, excess in drinking, dancing, and pleasure; against fornication, pandering, and adultery; against drunkenness and impurity. The Calvinist elders were agents of an enclosed system of belief and ideology; of control of the emotions, of a modest and decent lifestyle, of perseverance and self-discipline, and of a sober responsibility for one's own life and for others, within marriage, the family, and the community, as well as for society in general—in short, for a pure, honest and industrious society.

The Anglican, Lutheran, and Catholic confessional churches implemented discipline on a different theological and institutional basis, but the effects on the behavior and mentality of the faithful were quite similar. Like the Calvinistic consistories and synods, the widespread net of the Jesuits made a decisive contribution to the socially far-reaching dissemination of styles of thinking and behavior formed in the spirit of the modern period, among the princes and nobility as well as among the newly emergent educated elite of the state and also in the towns—although with less effect in the countryside. Particularly significant was the impetus given to middle-class society, into which the Jesuits introduced a "sufficiency of novelties, on the level of their family and of society, as well as on the manner in which religion is lived, such as to disquiet the upholders of tradition" (Louis Châtellier). In the Catholic world the agents of confessionalization were also working to Christianize society, to impose on each individual an obligation of self-exploration and self-guidance, a programmatic combination of religious introspection and a moral lifestyle within and for a fraternal Christian community—the "godly" family and nation. On the whole, all confessional churches represent a "modern

Christianity," though with different means and differing degrees of success, and they "appear, in a way, to be at the origin of the modern bourgeois spirit in Europe"—even the Catholic,[10] although its leaders from time to time like to display a marked antimodernism.

During the last decades the process of confessionalization, described here only in its main features, has been the object of an entire series of case studies and of many discussions among early modernists in Europe and North America. During these debates the paradigm—developed by German historians during the late 1970s and early 1980s, possessing a bias in favor of structural history—was modified and broadened considerably with regard to its psychological and cultural implications as well as with regard to denominations outside the three or four confessional churches and to the situation at the frontier of faith and in the borderlands, where different religions had to live together.[11] To my knowledge, however, up to now there have been no attempts to bring the European Jews into that picture. The paradigm of confessionalization could be applied to Jewish history in Europe from two perspectives: the *external,* inquiring about the impact of and the pressures the Jews had to endure from the confessionalization process within their Christian surrounding; and the *internal,* inquiring about the reaction of the Jewish congregations and communities to the dogmatic, institutional, social, and moral process of formation in Christianity. Did they react as did the Anabaptists,[12] who—though not a confessional church in a strict sense—nevertheless developed social and cultural mechanisms quite similar to confessional dominance? Or did the interior history of early modern Judaism follow only its own rules, separated or even isolated from fundamental processes like confessionalization within the Christian world?[13]

Confessionalization and Secularization

Religious, cultural, and social differentiation and modernization did not stop with confessionalization and its consequences, but went on to nonconfessional denominations, deists, freethinkers, and atheists. However influential the confessions were in shaping Europe, they never succeeded in attaining absolute dominance, and after the second half of the seventeenth century confessionalism was overcome step-by-step: The broad stream of internal Christian dissent, which the medieval Church was never really able to totally extinguish, resurfaced in the 1520s along with the Reformation. Though persecuted by Catholic as well as Protestant orthodoxy, these "Christians without a church" (Leszek Kołakowski)[14] survived the confessional era as an undercurrent and gained increasing influence by the end of the seventeenth century: the Baptists, who practiced the baptism of adults and made a strict separation of religious and secular matters; the Illuminati and the Spiritualists, who in the tradition of medieval mysticism were skeptical and even hostile to a Christendom of dogmas and gave priority to the internal experience of belief, up to the extreme of trancelike ecstasy; the Socinians and Anti-Trinitarians, who, like the early Christian Arians, rejected the doctrine of the Trinity and were, accordingly, particularly harshly persecuted as traitors to the state and as heretics. In countries like Poland, up to the end of the sixteenth century, and in the Dutch Republic, such groups were almost as well represented as the confessional churches.[15]

This diversification from outside was accompanied by a

diversification within the confessional churches: by Pietism, which placed emphasis on the inner piety of the heart, of the "simple" soul, among the Lutherans and in the lands of Reformation Europe; by Puritanism in Anglican England, which strengthened the communities and individual experiences of belief and which, after a revolutionary interlude in which the Puritans under the leadership of Oliver Cromwell actually took power, ensured that in 1689 all dissenters whose views diverged from the established Anglican Church obtained freedom of belief; and finally by Jansenism within the Catholic confessional church, which in Belgium and France, in particular, sought an Augustinian Renaissance for an ascetic and moral spiritualization of Christendom and fell into conflict with the papacy and the French crown. Finally, official theology itself began to cast religion within terms of philosophy and morals, and the attempt was made to establish a "moral religiosity of the conscience" (Johannes Kühn)[16] instead of the religion of revelation. Internal church demands for "universal reform," for the ever more extensive reforming of society and the individual—demands made by Johann Heinrich Alsted (1588–1638), Samuel Hartlib (1660–1662), Johannes Valentin Andreae (1586–1654) and Jan Amos Komensky or Comenius (1592–1670), among others—were integrated into the emergent trends of rationalism and empiricism in philosophy, the natural sciences, and medicine.[17] Added to this were the religious and spiritual forces of Judaism that, after the dissolution of the early symbiosis in Spain by the Catholic kings at the end of the fifteenth century, had largely progressed in isolation from Christian domination, but that had again gained substantial influence since the days of the great Dutch Jewish philosopher Baruch de Spinoza (1632–1677).[18]

To a considerable degree, these "new" ideas and attitudes

were rooted in concepts of the Renaissance and of human-
ism; they were undercurrents that had survived confessionalization. For, it was doubtless possible during the sixteenth
and early seventeenth centuries to think along tolerant and
secular lines—as notably documented by the astonishing
statement of a French lawyer from 1591, that "l'Estat et la
Religion n'ont rien de commune."[19] Apart from a short period during the reign of Henry IV in France, when the group
of Politiques set the tone, those secular ideas remained in
general circulation but without affecting the political and
social reality. That lack of effect changed only after the middle of the seventeenth century, when these ideas came to
the fore, affecting every aspect of everyday life. Unhampered
by the dictates of an authoritative religious orthodoxy, one
could interpret the world through observation and experience, in accordance with the criteria of common sense
and reason. At the same time, the pessimistic image of
the man of Confessional orthodoxy that resulted in the belief that man must be tamed by strict discipline and control of the state and church, became successively replaced
by a more optimistic concept of man. This more positive
view trusted the individual to take his interests—religious
as well as political and social ones—into his own hands,
thereby to promote not only his own but also the welfare of
the commonwealth.[20]

As we cannot discuss the long and contradictory process of
the vanishing of confessionalism in full, I conclude by recall-
ing the dialectical structure of the early modern process of
modernization that we have already observed in the history
of confessional minorities. On a more general level, we are
still dealing with the problem today; it is essential to keep in

mind this dialectic of religious and secular processes. As already mentioned, from its very beginnings, Latin Europe developed a tendency for secularization and for intellectual as well as political autonomy. Even early modern confessionalism did not suspend this tendency. Thus, in the early modern period, resacralization in the wake of confessionalism and long-term secularization did not exclude each other. On the contrary, in competition with confessionalism, secularization gained a new dynamic and profited from the power of confessionalization. By transferring a formerly religious emphasis into the secular sphere, secularization even profited from the preceding confessionalization, whose formerly religious emphasis endorsed the new secular forces and gave them a specific legitimacy.

On this basis, the Enlightenment's postulation of the *emergence of man from his self-imposed disenfranchisement*, this disenfranchisement being understood as the "inability to service his understanding without the guidance of another" (Kant) was by no means a simple rebellion against religion, but to a considerable degree the product of processes rooted in religion itself and its pertinence to the secular sphere, characteristic of the Latin European type of civilization. In conclusion, this postulate might be best illustrated by a well-known symbolic representation of European culture (which, as are so many manifestations of Christian theory and culture, is actually of Jewish origin): the dove of peace. The traditional representation of peace by the dove was greatly resacralized when the Thirty Years' War came to an end and the Peace of Westphalia established a new order between the states and the confessions. It was based on the maxim "pax sit Christiana": peace should be not only between confessions, states, and political powers, but also between mankind and God. And such was also exactly the message of the dove-representation of the West-phalian Peace: the Dove carrying a laurel branch to Noah's Ark, to assure the reconciliation of man and God.[21]

Right up to its use in the peace movement at the end of the twentieth century, the dove as a representation of peace underwent profound changes, intellectually as well as aesthetically. And there is no doubt that this change must be described as secularization, not in the sense of cutting down all former religious connotations, but of transforming the religious emphasis and energy into the secular context and giving the new secular meaning a specific legitimating. We shall return to this point in chapter 4, when we consider the political and religious conflicts of the late sixteentth and first half of the seventeenth centuries and identify the means by which Europe was able to overcome the chaos of self-destruction.

III Migration and Minorities

The Early Modern Confessional Migration—
a Typological Approach

Migration and minorities were constitutive elements of European history well before the industrialization and urbanization of the nineteenth and twentieth centuries and they shaped the social and cultural profile of European civilization profoundly. Since the Middle Ages they were key to the growth of industry and commerce, especially for the diffusion of technical, institutional, or organizational innovations in manufacturing, financing, or distribution. Towns in particular were thus enabled to adapt human capital to changing economic circumstances.[1] At the same time, migration had a strong impact on European culture and was widely responsible for the diffusion of ideas, concepts, and manifestations of art and literature. Even socially—though not without tension and friction—migration and minorities shaped the civilization of Old Europe to a greater extent than historians or social scientist, thinking in categories of the nation states of the nineteenth and twentieth have been ready to admit. This effect was particularly true for the commercial and industrial centers of towns, especially urban centers. In addition, some rural areas profited from migration, particularly in the eastern and southeastern parts of Europe and some of the marsh districts of England where the superior drainage techniques of Dutch immigrants paved the way for settlement and agriculture.[2] With regard to migration, as in many other aspects, European societies of the early twenty-first century are closer to early modern societies (especially the early modern urban centers, than to the national-state societies of the nineteenth century. Consequently, early modern history may help us to understand today's situation better and to open up perspectives toward future models of conviviality.[3]

In this section I shall not focus on the ordinary, everyday type of migration well researched by demographers and economic and social historians, but on the extraordinary type. Even among the everyday, different types of migration can be distinguished: for example, betterment and subsistence migration as a result of a local or regional subsistence crisis, or migration caused by the desire to improve one's or one's family's economic and social position by moving into urban places with better opportunities. Within this approach, research has focused on the "normal" fluctuation between town and countryside as well as between individual towns and cities. We know nearly everything about the structure and consequences of this Old European migration. We know that large and medium-size cities, because of their high mortality rates, could not have survived without their very high ratio of migrants. We know about the hierarchy of places associated with immigration: from village, to small and medium-size towns, and finally to the big cities, and that only a very small proportion of migrants moved in the opposite direction.[4] We know about remigration to places of origin; about seasonal migration, and the migration of people with specific skills (such as the Italian chimney cleaners to the northern countries) and so forth.

The following is not concerned with this everyday migration known to almost all world civilizations, but instead with the exceptional waves of long-distance trans-European migration, launched by religious and ecclesiastical formation, characteristic of early modern Europe, and, as we shall see, a source of dynamism and an engine of social change. Forerunners in the late Middle Ages notwithstanding, this extraordinary wave of long-distance, transcontinental migration reached its characteristic force and societal and cultural energy during the first centuries of the early modern period, starting with the "grand migration alpine Vaudoise"[5] of the late fifteenth century; followed by the Protestant refuge of the sixteenth century, mainly Dutch and Walloons, and to a lesser extent, French and Italians; by a second wave during the seventeenth century—the Austrian and Bohemian Protestants of the early, the Huguenots of the late seventeenth century—and finally, the Salzburgian exiles of the early eighteenth century.[6] Last but not least, the Jewish Sephardic migration from the Iberian Peninsula of the sixteenth and seventeenth centuries belongs to that category.[7] This Jewish migration is excellently researched, but usually isolated from the movements within the Christian populations just mentioned. Nonetheless, the pushing and pulling factors were the same and, as I shall maintain here, so were the many consequences of the new settlements.

Demographers, if touching upon the problem at all,[8] usually regard this refugee movement as a mixed type or subtype of "normal" migration; that is, as a mixture of betterment and subsistence migration.[9] In the following I shall assess this extraordinary long-distance migration not as one part of everyday migration, but in a wider perspective that considers not only the demographic and economic factors but also the legal, mental, and cultural factors, especially religious ones.

In this perspective the migratory waves just mentioned must be characterized as manifestations of a specific type within the Old European migration scene, for which I have termed the expression *confessional migration* (*Konfessionsmigration*)[10], because of their common origin in the process of "confessionalization" of European states and societies, (already touched upon in chapters 1 and 2). Confessional migration does not refer only to the religious causes and motives of migration but rather to the special conditions of settlement within the host countries as well as to the way in which the innovative impulses prevailed or were forestalled. Especially in the German empire, where the "cuius regio eius religio" (he who controls the area controls the religion) principle was established, the religion or "confession" of the migrants determined not only the religious and ecclesiastical but also the legal, social, cultural, and even the economic conditions under which the "religious refugees" could live and work.[11]

During the long-term process of confessional migration from the late fifteenth to the middle of the eighteenth century several hundred thousand, probably altogether one million people left their home countries. As there are no statistics—owing to the time period as well as to the clandestine character of the emigration—we shall never obtain reliable figures. Reasonable estimates based on regional or local statistical data collected mainly by the magistrates of the host societies might come to the following numbers for the distinct waves in chronological order: several thousand for the "migration alpine Vaudoise" since the fifteenth century, approximately 5,000 persons to the Luberon region north of Aix-en-Provence only, several hundred to southern Italy and Germany; from 100,000 to 150,000 for the Dutch and Walloon Protestant refugees of the sixteenth century; from 100,000 to 120,000 for the Bohemian and Austrian Protestants of the early seventeenth century; from 250,000 to 300,000 for the Huguenots of the late seventeenth century; and 20,000 for the Salzburgians of the eighteenth century. In addition to these major waves, some smaller waves were launched during the sixteenth century—Catholic migrants from Belgian cities, which became Calvinistic during the 1570s and 1580s (still poorly researched); Protestants from Italy, especially from Lucca; and the Marian Exiles from England during the 1550s[12]—which, altogether, might have added some 10,000 people to the number of early modern confessional migrants. And, starting in the late sixteenth century, and with an apogee during the decades in the middle of the following century, from 100,000 to 150,000 Jewish refugees had to leave Spain and Portugal, although only a relatively small number settled in Western and Central Europe; several hundred settled in Hamburg and in London, and from 2,000 to 2,500 settled in Amsterdam.[13]

Compared with the present-day numbers of migrants these are modest figures, especially as the confessional migration extended itself across around two centuries. Nevertheless, these numbers had as great an impact on the host societies as do the statistically larger movement of the present. During the sixteenth century in the German cities of Frankfort, Wesel, and Emden, the migrants reached a proportion of 20 percent (in Emden during several years even 50 percent of the inhabitants). At Leiden the Flemish and Walloon immigrants were 53.7 percent of the people marrying during one year; and by 1700, 20 percent of the inhabitants of Berlin were of Huguenot origin.[14] Considering their economic, social, and cultural activities—and especially their obvious deviance in ecclesiastical and religious matters—there can be no doubt that these stranger colonies posed a great challenge to their host societies.

As the Dutch and Walloon refugees of Calvinist or Reformed confession moved to Lutheran, Catholic (for example, Cologne and Aix-la-Chapelle in northwestern Germany), or Anglican places, they formed a religious and ecclesiastical dissenting minority comparable to that of the Jewish settlement. In some cases—as the Sephardim in London up to the middle of the seventeenth century, or the Calvinist refugees in Catholic regions—even in their places of refuge, the migrants had to conceal their religion, and with it, a central part of their identity. Consequently the Dutch and Walloon settlement of the Lower Rhine area organized their religious life through underground churches, which they called "churches under the cross"; that is to say, under the cross of permanent danger of disclosure and persecution. Primarily because of this religious deviance the migrants and their descendants in most places had to live for generations as strangers, granted, with a more or less stable legal status, but culturally and socially segregated from the majority of the host society.

In consequence, the settlements of the confessional immigrants confronted western and northern European societies for the first time with the problem of dissenting migrant minorities *within* Christian society itself. And vice versa: for the first time, Christian minorities in the very center of European civilization had to cope on a greater scale with the experience of being culturally and ideologically identified as *others* and *strangers*. The vulnerable identity of "peregrine" was no longer restricted to the Jews or, in some border regions of Europe, to Muslims. It is not so much the number of displaced people, but this fundamental change in the history and the social, legal, and cultural status of minorities that makes the confessional migration central to the early modern process of transformation. Confessional migration brought new dynamism and new structures into the traditional migration scene. Even more important, it functioned as a strong agent of social change and—if one dares apply this model any longer—of modernization, not only with regard to its demographic, economic and social, but also to its cultural impact and outlook. Like many phenomena of the sixteenth and early seventeenth centuries, confessional migration occupied an intermediate position between the migration typical of the Middle Ages and the migration pattern characteristic of the later early modern period.

The Early Migration from Habsburg Territories of the Netherlands and Iberia: Chronology, Motives, Numbers, Places, and Condition of Settlement

The most prominent manifestation of the confessional migration type is the French Huguenot migration of the late seventeenth century. Its prominence is mainly due to the effective memory of and accounts by their descendants, which made them a kind of European *lieu de mémoire* understood as a focal point of collective memory and identity.[15] Yet in several respects the impact of the earlier waves was more decisive for the history of European transformation. In the following I shall focus on two main currents of this early wave, which actually can be treated as two branches of one movement: the branch of Dutch and Walloon Protestant refugees from the Habsburg Netherlands and the branch of the Sephardim or Spaniolen refugees from Spain and Portugal. Both branches were launched by the long-term cultural and political formation processes in Spain and the Habsburg lands in general, starting in the Iberian world well into the fifteenth century (that is, in a pre-Reformation context), but culminating during the reign of Philip II in a powerful catholic confessionalization—or, in the case of the Netherlands, in a desperate attempt to enforce it by military intervention and all-embracing terror. There are also parallels in the way Protestants and Jews responded to the challenge of forced migration that deserve the attention of historians.

To discuss the Calvinist and Sephardic migration in a comparative perspective allows us to overcome at a small but important point the isolation of Jewish and Christian history, respectively, by bringing them into a common, comparative perspective. I hope that at the same time this setting will open further insights into the Christian-Jewish relationship and perhaps also into paths and instruments of social or cultural osmosis and transfer between both. To compare Jewish and Christian minority status and minority life gives us a reliable indicator of the extent of otherness or participation of the Jews in the society and the culture of Latin Europe respectively. As I am not an expert in Jewish history of that period, I can only try to offer an initial approach in a comparative perspective—a perspective, I acknowledge, that raises more questions than it answers.

The emigration out of the Habsburg Netherlands was a process of nearly one hundred years with periodically intensified waves differing in both their social composition and economic character. The emigration began in the 1530s as a consequence of the anti-Protestant policy of Charles V. It reached its climax between 1567 and 1590 at the time of the military intervention of the Spaniards with the duke of Alba (1567–1573) and Alexandro Farnese (1578–1592), respectively, as commander and governor-in-chief. It continued, albeit with decreasing intensity, well into the first quarter of the seventeenth century. At the beginning, almost all the emigrants were Anabaptists. From the late 1540s onward, the emigration was increasingly dominated by Calvinists, although there were also Lutherans among them. Even small groups of Catholics emigrated temporarily, especially from Flanders and Brabant during the years of the Calvinist republics, for example, in Ghent and Antwerp.[16] Estimates of the size of the emigration vary considerably, ranging from fifty thousand to half a million. It seems realistic to speak of just under 100,000 refugees, who left their home country temporarily or forever.[17] The main area of emigration was the southern Netherlands, which were recaptured and re-Catholicized in the 1570s and 1580s. The inhabitants of the northern provinces only took part in the early waves of emigration. Most of them returned beginning in the 1570s onward. The early migration wave was dominated by smaller merchants, craftsmen, journeymen, and paid laborers, mainly from textile manufacturing. In the 1560s the proportion of wealthy merchants (involved, for example, in the Baltic grain trade), of entrepreneurs, and of financiers increased steadily. It reached its peak in the 1580s, when Alexander Farnese recaptured Brussels, Ghent, and Antwerp, the great commercial and manufacturing centers of the south. Immigration areas included parts of northern France, England, Germany (especially the northwestern border region to the Netherlands), parts of Switzerland, Poland, the Scandinavian kingdoms (above all, Sweden), as well as, since the late sixteenth century, the newly founded northern Dutch Republic. However, the great bulk of the refugees settled in the big cities: in Amsterdam, London, Hamburg, Emden (at that time one of the busiest harbors in all Europe), Frankfurt am Main, and even catholic Cologne.

Amsterdam, London, and Hamburg were also the favorite places of refuge for the Jewish branch of the confessional migration.[18] If one also takes into account the traditional

settlements of the Ashkenazi in Frankfurt and Emden and—
owing to war pressures—their migration into many of the
smaller towns in the lower Rhine area (for exmple, Cleve and
Wesel),[19] then the geographical overlapping in the settlement
area of the two minorities becomes obvious. In many, if not
most places of Protestant refuge there existed also a Jewish
minority, mostly smaller, but not substantially so: approximately 650 Jewish to 1,000 (later on 2,000) Christian refugees in the case of Hamburg and London; 2,000 Sephardim
and several hundred Ashkenazi to several thousand Protestant refugees from the southern provinces in the case of Amsterdam.[20] The motives for leaving the home country and for
choosing a particular place of refuge were also similar, although the motives and character of the Dutch and Walloon
emigration have been disputed vehemently by Dutch and
Belgian historians. Actually, it seems reasonable to accept
that in case of the Protestant as well as the Jewish refuge,
motives were diffuse and mixed; that is to say, flight from
religious persecution did not exclude flight for economic and
political reasons. The latter are especially obvious for the
1585 emigration from Antwerp, which was based on a treaty
between the city and the besieging Spanish army, granting
free emigration to everybody. Consequently this wave took
on the character of a large-scale business transfer of entrepreneurial and commercial firms and their employees.

Christian as well as Jewish entrepreneurs, bankers, or
commercial family firms were eager to keep up their international network and tried to place members in the commercial and financial centers of the Continent, whatever
their confession and ecclesiastical policy.[21] Since, with regard to religion, the best places for the Sephardic migration
would have been the well-established Jewish congregations
in North Africa and the Near East, it seems obvious that

Hamburg, London, and Amsterdam, were attractive to the Iberian Jews not primarily for religious reasons, but for the economic opportunities they offered.[22] The same is true for the Calvinist Dutch refugees migrating to Catholic Cologne, Lutheran Hamburg or Frankfurt, and to a certain extent also to London or one of the other cities in Anglican England. In all of these cities and regions, the Calvinist Netherlanders had the restricted status of a religious minority, in the same way, or in nearly the same way, as the Jews. And the host societies—the leaders of their Lutheran, Catholic, or Anglican churches in particular, but also the civic authorities—handled both religious minorities in nearly the same manner. There were periods of strong popular pressure against strangers, especially in the decades around 1600, when in Hamburg and Frankfurt popular protests erupted against the Christian as well as the Jewish minority and the magistrates had to end their liberal stranger policy.[23] Owing to popular pressure headed by the Lutheran ministers in Frankfurt as well as in Hamburg, the new Calvinist as well as the Jewish minority settlements had to leave the city several times for the nearby smaller towns outside the city's jurisdiction. In the case of Hamburg, the colonies were temporarilly transferred to Altona or Stade, which were under the jurisdiction of neighboring territorial rulers—who, like the city magistrates, were interested in the economic skills of the strangers, but were not so dependent on popular sentiments and pressures as their urban counterparts.[24]

These parallels, however, should not hide one decisive difference: the popular protests against the minority settlements also included violence against Christians. During riots of craftsmen in Catholic Cologne the dyeing kettles and other tools of the Protestant Dutch entrepreneurs were smashed. Fatal violence and murder, however, took place only against Jews: for example, during the riot of Fincenz Fettmilch in Frankfurt, which was rooted in a general popular opposition to the liberal policy of the magistrate toward the Dutch and Walloon immigration, but nevertheless ended in a murderous pogrom against the Jewish ghetto and its Ashkenazi community that had been established for generations.[25] In contrast the new Sephardic colony at Hamburg was never confronted with this kind of violence.

Though the city authorities were protecting the stranger colonies for largely economic reasons, in Lutheran Hamburg or Frankfurt as well as in Catholic Cologne or Aix-la-Chapelle and Anglican London they were firmly concerned with preventing any influence of the stranger's dissenting belief on the ecclesiastical and confessional status of the city, or—in England—of the realm. In some places (notably in Aix-la-Chapelle, which temporarily turned from Catholic to Calvinist belief), there was an actual danger of a conversion of the church system by the Calvinist minority; with regard to the Jews, however, such a development was totally hypothetical and the Christian authorities were only concerned with possible conversions of individuals. Any other concerns, not only of the magistrates, but also of the burgher community as a whole, was relevant for the Jewish minority as well as for the Christian dissenters: the issue of dogmatic and moral "purity" of their respective city, which must be protected from desecration and staining by Jews as well as by dogmatic and impure "heretics." Although hard to evaluate in their psychological dimension, those ritual representations were in any case of great concern in the traditional context of the Old European city communities. At least during the sixteenth century, the idea of urban purity had some influence on the circumstances of the religious minorities within their host societies.[26]

Aside from these religious and sacred concerns the minority policy of the English as well as that of the German authorities was guided by the desire to prevent a possible destabilization of the social and political order, which at the end of the sixteenth century generally was under great pressure. In England the complex and vulnerable Elizabethan ecclesiastical settlement seemed to be at stake: the Calvinist stranger churches and their Presbyterian self-government could strengthen the Puritan movement in church and Parliament against the episcopal structure of the Church of England and the royal prerogative in politics. The political and constitutional situation in Germany was even more complex under the "cuius regio eius religio" maxim of the Peace of Augsburg, giving the princes as well as the magistrates of the imperial cities the choice between Lutheran and Catholic confessions of their respective territorial or city churches (*Stadt-* or *Landeskirchen*). On this legal basis, imperial lawyers (*Reichsjuristen*) and political theorists developed the fundamental maxim of "religio vinculum societatis" (uniformity of religion is indispensable for civic order and peace), by which the toleration of dissenting minorities was excluded.[27] In Germany, as Calvinists were excluded from the Peace of Augsburg, magistrates tolerating Calvinist minorities took a double risk: of violating the commonsense principle of religious uniformity in the city (and by this of provoking protests and even riots by the clergy and the burgher community): and of violating the constitution and the laws of the Empire. Consequently, every magistrate who tolerated them risked being sued at the imperial courts or at least losing the grace of the emperor—a real political danger, especially in Frankfurt, the imperial city and site of coronation, but also to a city like Hamburg. During the decades of constitutional, confessional, and political crisis in the empire around 1600,[28] the argument that tolerance for Calvinists would be contrary to the peace of religion and to the loyalty due the emperor[29] was not always a simple expression of xenophobia: frequently it was sound political advice. Contrary to the Calvinist minority, the Jewish settlement in Frankfurt profited from the close legal and constitutional bonds of the imperial city to the emperor: After the pogrom connected with the Fettmilch rebellion, in which the Jewish quarter was burned down and the future of the settlement seemed at stake, an imperial commission investigated the events, brought the responsible persons to trial, and introduced a new statute by which Jewish life in Frankfurt enjoyed a certain amount of stability for the next generations.[30]

The economic interest of the magistrates or the political elite in favor of the migrants and the economic or social opposition of the population against the migrants notwithstanding, conditions of settlement depended primarily on the religious and ecclesiastical status of the host society. In western and northern Europe the religious and ecclesiastical framework for the stranger colonies was settled quickly and more smoothly than in central Europe. Indeed, in the northern Netherlands the Calvinist refugees met with no restrictions at all, as the public church of the republic was a Calvinist one. And, as Dutch society was multiconfessional or even pluralistic, tolerance also prevailed with regard to Jewish service. In Anglican England and in Lutheran Sweden royal privileges provided a clearly defined framework in which the Netherlanders could establish their own Calvinist congregations without problems for the confession of the natives—a model, which by the middle of the seventeenth century was extended to the Sephardic community of London.[31] In contrast to these quick and clear solutions, the situation of the German settlements was complicated and complex—confessionally, politically, economically, and socially. Because of the heavy impact of confessionalization in the wake of the "cuius regio eius religio" principle, which privileged Lutherans and Catholics exclusively, Catholic or Lutheran German cities and territories were extremely hostile to the Calvinist migrants, who were regarded as religious strangers or even enemies. Consequently, the Calvinist refugee colonies from the Netherlands became more or less isolated minorities without connubial or full civil rights. Even their ecclesiastical basis was weak and they were often forbidden to have public or even private services within the boundaries of the respective city. Although by the middle of the seventeenth century, at the latest, their descendants had to be regarded as Germans, in cities like Cologne, Hamburg, and Frankfurt, even a century later, they were still considered a special group, distinct from the "natives." Owing to religious and cultural differences, the immigration of Calvinist, quite similar to that of the Jewish refugees, resulted in segregation and isolation from the Christian host societies.[32] Even well into the nineteenth century, when Goethe wrote his autobiographical text *Dichtung und Wahrheit*, he described the Calvinist or reformed congregation of his native city Frankfurt as a special group: "Die sogenannten Reformirten bildeten, wie auch an anderen Orten die Refugiés, eine ausgezeichnete Classe" (a distinct and isolated class).[33]

The Reaction of the Calvinist and Sephardic Migrants to Religious and Social Segregation

The reaction of the two migrant groups to their respective cultural and religious minority status in the foreign, ideologically hostile society was quite similar, even with regard to the instruments and social or cultural functions they developed in reaction. Like the Sephardi congregation, which on the basis of the notion of *nação* (nation) developed a strong exclusive identity,[34] the Calvinist refugees usually formed two different communities or (the Dutch expression) *naties*: the one for the French-speaking Walloon, the other for the Dutch-speaking Nederduits or Flemish migrants. Though normally the exclusiveness was less severe than in the case of the Jewish congregation, the combination of religious and regional or "national" identity was the same. Similar parallels can be seen in the strong structures of family and business networks, and in the system of information transmission and assistance, which was decisive for the direction and logistics of the migration of individuals and individual families and their reception and early integration into the migrant colony. Characteristic of both minority groups was also a specific awareness of the instability of the political situation, not only on the local and regional level, but also in the international context of the changing constellations within the European system of power states.

The most distinctive feature in the profile of the Calvinist minorities was their model of church government. While it was rooted in Calvin's theology,[35] it got its actual and exceptional meaning only from the refugee and minority churches. It was based on the revolutionary theory that each congregation in itself was a church in the strict sense. Thus the Calvinist refugees neither needed the global church organization of the Catholics, nor the *Landes-* or *Staatskirchen*, the territorial or national churches of the Lutherans or Anglicans. An ecclesiological model prived ideal for the everyday situation of the migrants: each of the Calvinist minority churches together with its refugee colony was ruled by a church council or "presbytery," formed by the pastors together with twelve elders, chosen out of the male members. A second council, the diaconate, chosen after a similar procedure, was responsible for poor relief and charity, health care, and for the hospitals. The rule of the presbytery extended to all questions of interior government of the congregation *and* its exterior relations—with the civic authorities of the host society as well as with other congregations or foreign authorities in the region and in Europe generally. The most prominent concern of the elders, however, was the control of belief and behavior of the individual members of the congregation. To enforce the moral and dogmatic standards, the presbytery had a variety of instruments at its disposal: private or public admonition and penitence, cutting short of poor relief, temporary exclusion of the sacraments, and—the last and most severe—banishment or excommunication. As all discussion and decisions of the weekly sessions were taken down in the minutes of the presbyteries, which are mostly preserved from the sixteenth to the nineteenth century, we are well informed about the specific objectives and standards of these church disciplines and their changes over the centuries.[36]

The differences in legal and social status as well as in the religious life and organization of the congregation notwithstanding, the profile of the Calvinist and Jewish Sephardic congregation had several features in common.[37] First and foremost, the energetic struggle of the governors for moral and dogmatic "purity" of the congregation in the case of the Christian minority congregations, expressed by excommunication. Distinctive to Emden during the 1550s[38] was exclusion of the nonrepentant sinner from eucharistic celebrations, to prevent the holy congregation from being besmirched and disgraced before God. This idea of "purity" went together with strong pressure for internal integration in dogma and belief and correspondent intervention against dissenting opinions: for example, the excommunication of Adrian van Haemstede, minister of the Dutch refugee churches in London and Emden[39] in the case of the Calvinists; or the famous Spinoza excommunication in the case of the Amsterdam Sephardic congregation. Parallels are also obvious with the exterior policy of segregation or even isolation from the host societies in religious as well as in secular matters (for example, the prohibition from going to court) to minimize possible friction with the host society. Complementary to these separatist tendencies was a strong pressure for internal social integration and coherence within the families—between husband and wife and between parents and children, in mutual direction, in which obedience of the children corresponds to the responsibility of the parents, especially regarding education and schooling—extending to the neighborhoods and to the congregation as a whole. And finally, closely connected with the idea of social and dogmatic coherence and of the purity of the holy community, strong emphasis was put on the enforcement of the rules and moral standards of matrimony, matrimonial life, and sexual behavior.[40]

Given those similarities and parallels, it seems appropriate to raise the question whether, to what extent, and on which theological or ethical basis the Jewish minority congregations (and European Jews in general) participated in the fundamental process of discipline and social control, characteristic of the civilization of Latin Europe since the late Middle Ages and key to shaping Europe's modernity.

A Dialectic of Traditionalism and Progress— Considerations on Long-term Economic and Cultural Consequences

Indisputably, confessional migration and many of the institutions, functions, cultural representations, and perspectives of the early modern confessional minorities are part of the traditional cultural and societal system of the pre-modern era. This is true for the early modern confessional national, territorial, or city-state, and its struggle for religious uniformity, which was responsible for the expulsion of the refugees as well as for the restrictive conditions of their settlements. And it is also true for the complementary eagerness of the minority congregations for exclusiveness and near total internal integration: their ideal of ideological and moral purity with correspondent instruments of disciplining their members, the high value placed on matrimony, the family, and family networks together with smoothly functioning neighborhoods—functioning not only with regard to assistance, but also to control. But traditionalism did not at all mean stagnation or immobilization. Here I can refer to a statement of Yosef Kaplan, who gave the complex situation of early modern development an unsurpassable formulation. In evaluating the intellectual ties between Jews and Christians in seventeenth-century Amsterdam, which were not at all "based on a universalistic, rationalist ideology, which legitimized the neutralisation of religious differences," he uncovers the dialectical nature of the process of change in early modern societies. The Amsterdam experience "shows how far traditionalism and modernism are from being unidimensional, and it demonstrates how simplistic it would be to see the distinction between traditional and modern societies as a dichotomy."[41] This observation of the social and intellectual profile of the Sephardic colony in Amsterdam matches similar observations of the Calvinist minority settlements. In the following, greater detail will be offered in regard to the impulses of the Calvinist minorities in the lower Rhineland region for long-term economic and social development and in regard to a specific expression of their social and religious identity.

In the medieval and early modern period, socioeconomic impulses as a rule were connected with migration as the dominant instrument for transfer and dissemination of skills, technical expertise, and innovations in general.[42] In the case of the confessional migrants of the sixteenth and seventeenth centuries those innovative impulses were especially strong and long-lasting. This strength was first of all the consequence of their superior skill and knowledge. Coming from the most economically advanced parts of Europe, the refugees introduced to their host countries several effective innovations in commercial and financing practices, manufacturing techniques, and forms of labor organization. The diffusion of these economic innovations over Europe, which normally occurred slowly, was considerably accelerated and intensified by confessional migration. Consequently confessional immigration meant significant economic and social advantages for the host countries, whereas the emigration from the Iberian Peninsula and from the southern provinces of the Netherlands weakened the commercial and industrial basis of the Spanish empire considerably.[43]

The economic impulses for the host societies resulted less from the purely quantitative population increase than from the extensive business connections of the Calvinist and Jewish merchants and financiers and from the skilled manufacturing techniques of the Dutch and Walloon craftsmen and entrepreneurs, mainly in the textile, metal, and luxury sectors (gold, silver, jewelry, silk, sugar, tapestries, and so on). England and Sweden, which had just experienced the rise of a protonational system in commerce and industry, profited enormously from the Dutch and Walloon migration. As I shall describe in more detail below, the same was true for the traditional commercial centers in western and northern Germany. Doubtless, however, it was the northern Dutch

Republic that derived the greatest economic, social, and cultural advantage from the migrants, both from the Calvinist-Christian migrants from the southern provinces (which remained under Spanish rule), and from the Sephardic-Jewish exiles from the Iberian Peninsula. The famous *handel op de vijand*, the Dutch and north German trade with Spanish territories,[44] which—though greatly disparaged by politicians and pamphleteers—contributed decisively in the early years to the financial basis for the Dutch warfare against Spain, was organized to a considerable extent through the network of refugee merchants. Later on, the extraordinary economic boom of the republic's *Gouden Eeuw* (Golden Era) was to no small extent based on the activities of the Christian and Jewish refugees from the southern Netherlands and Spain or Portugal respectively.

Apart from these economic and social connections, the extraordinary impulses for innovations and economic as well as social and cultural dynamism resulted from their specific status as confessional minorities. During the process of confessionalization[45] religious minorities underwent in Latin European societies a unique process of formation in dogma, morals, behavior, and cultural as well as social self-understanding or identity, that, together with the complementary process of confessionalization within the host society formed the precondition for their exceptional dynamism—not the least in economic matters. This success was obvious especially within the German context, where the confessionalization process was more deeply rooted than in other European countries.

In this context, the situation of the refugee colonies as described—their segregation and self-isolation, their traditionalism in norms of thinking and behavior—did not result in stagnation and social backwardness. On the contrary, because of their dogmatic exclusiveness, their social segregation, and their abstention from political participation, the refugee colonies in some regions produced an extraordinary economic, cultural, and even societal dynamism. In London, Hamburg, and Frankfurt, and also in some medium-size cities, the Calvinist as well as the Jewish minorities not only contributed extensively to the early modern economic growth of the respective cities; they were also responsible for the introduction of new techniques and methods in commerce and industry. And it was thanks to these effective techniques that a modern economy appeared in these cities earlier than it did elsewhere. How important these impulses from the confessional minorities actually were becomes obvious when we consider the total failure of the Calvinist settlements in the Catholic cities of the Lower Rhineland. Although the events in Cologne and Aix-la-Chapelle were quite different,[46] at the beginning of the seventeenth century it was certain that—in contrast to Hamburg, Frankfurt, London, or Amsterdam—economic pragmatism and limited tolerance did not prevail in either of these Catholic cities. The coalition of early modern confessionalism and the traditional, antiliberal economic mentality of the craftsmen that ultimately had been defeated in the Lutheran cities, succeeded in the Catholic ones. The refugees, and with them numerous native Protestants (among them more entrepreneurs and great merchants than average), left the inhospitable cities. Some of them went to Frankfurt or small territorial towns of the Rhineland. Others, however, transferred their economic sites into the countryside, founding new economic centers outside of the old manufacturing and mercantile cities.[47]

Compared with the traditional urban economy, these rural or semiurban centers were characterized by modern production techniques and more liberal business structures. There were, for example, the textile manufacturing and trade centers in Burtscheid, situated directly outside the gates of Aix-la-Chapelle in the territory of a free imperial Cistercian abbey, and the iron production centers in the Gemünd and Schleiden valleys or the brass manufacturing centers in the Vichttal, partly in the territory of Jülich, partly in subdomains, above all in Stolberg and in the domain of the imperial abbey of Cornelimünster. We may also include the textile production in Monschau (important in the eighteenth century), as well as the textile and paper production in the region of Düren, which was also founded and run by Protestant merchants and entrepreneurs outside of the old urban elites. Krefeld developed similar socioeconomic structures, but on a different socioconfessional basis. The community was politically monopolized by Calvinists, whereas the economic innovations and the entrepreneurial activities (here mainly linen and silk manufacturing) were organized by immigrated Mennonites.

And it was here, in the Lower Rhine region, where, within the Calvinist confessional minority, based in the migrant movements of the sixteenth century, the rise of an "early modern commercial and entrepreneurial bourgeoisie" (*frühmodernes Wirtschaftsbürgertum*) took place beginning in the late seventeenth century. This bourgeoisie was characterized not so much by the specific Weberian "Calvinist ethic" and inner-worldly asceticism (a result of predestination dogma), but by a specific refugee theology[48] and by their minority status in general. This claim might be illustrated by a short glance at the situation of the copper industry of Stolberg, a small hamlet in the neighborhood of Aix-la-Chapelle, and its entrepreneurial elite. This industry was imported by migrants from the southern Netherlands into the imperial city of Aix-la-Chapelle and transferred into the nearby countryside after the Protestant community was expelled from the city, owing to the entry of the Spanish army and subsequent re-Catholization in the early seventeenth century.[49] The expulsion from the imperial city, where the Protestants had dominated the council for several decades, meant a general exclusion from political participation—with the consequence that the public activities of the minority elite was restricted to the economy and the church community for coming generations. As a result, they devoted most of their time to ecclesiastical matters. Immediately after their removal from Aix-la-Chapelle they established private church services in their "copper manors" (*Kupferhöfe*). Later they financed and managed the construction of church buildings, and they nearly dominated to exclusivity the presbyteries, by which the minority churches were governed. And, as both church activities and economic activities were based on strong family structures, shaped by the experience of migration, the existence of this early Protestant entrepreneurial bourgeoisie was founded on the triangle of family-church-economy. On the one hand, their economic activities as well as their efforts within the Protestant congregation guaranteed the material and spiritual stability of the families within these economic elites. On the other hand the families supported the activities in the church and the economy and thus guaranteed the continuity of the individual firms as well as the economic and social monopoly of the Protestant entrepreneurial families as a whole. This reciprocity is expressed by the structure of the guild, under which these Protestant entrepreneurs had been formally united since 1669. In contrast to traditional guilds, this guild was not primarily concerned with the regulation of techniques; rather, it was a kind of family cartel that secured the monopoly of the small circle of old Protestant "copper master" families.

The corporate principles in the administration of churches and businesses as well as the family-centred organization of ecclesiastical and economic corporations (both typical of early modern society) indicate that this "early modern commercial bourgeoisie" was a phenomenon of transition between the corporate burgher elite of the urban centers of the Middle Ages and early modern period on the one hand and the individualistic, liberal business bourgeoisie of the late eighteenth and especially the nineteenth centuries on the other. Because of their religious minority status, which excluded them from political participation, the economic entrepreneurial elite no longer had the global capacity to hold political power on the city or town councils. At the same time, the exclusion signified liberation from involvement in the feudal structures of the traditional society. This liberation protected the Calvinist minority elite from the so-called (self)-betrayal of the bourgeoisie[50] and its transfer of capital from commerce and industry into feudal rents, estates, and elevation to noble status. The commitment to commercial and entrepreneurial capital and activities without alternative, together with the strong church and family bonds, enabled the Protestant entrepreneurs to build up large firms independent from urban facilities and thus to establish a new form of burgher existence outside of the towns. Consequently, they became important to the transformation of the traditional urban burgher society into the modern bourgeois society that developed in the Rhineland in the late eighteenth century—clearly earlier than in other parts of Germany.

As the economic elite of the Jewish minority developed a quite similar profile—exclusion from public offices, but leading positions in the congregation, social commitment, strong family circles, and so on—it was able to forge a similar path to modernity. In contrast to the entrepreneurs and merchants of the Calvinist minorities, however, whose economic chances and political possibilities were widened enormously when the religious restrictions of the ancien régime tumbled down, the elite of the Jewish minority were only confronted with new obstacles and animosities; thus their life in the modern bourgeois society of the nineteenth and twentieth centuries was not substantially easier than it had been during the early modern period. But that is an issue that would require another chapter to discuss.

My second and final reflection on the long-term impact of the European confessional migration is concerned with a specific cultural and symbolic representation of the refugees and its possible consequences for the differences in attitude toward minorities and strangers within the respective European societies. Here I can give only brief observations. At the apogee of confessionalism, many of the Calvinist refugees had the experience of being strangers and peregrines in a manner that, up to that point, had been restricted nearly exclusively to Jews. A striking example is the case of the London stranger churches presided over by the Polish nobleman and reformer Jan Lasky (Johannes a Lasco). After the succession of the Catholic queen Mary, these congregations had to leave London in wintertime for the Continent, but were hindered by Lutheran pastors and their flocks from entering towns and cities in northern Germany. Only after an odyssey of several weeks were they accepted in Frankfurt, at least for a few years.[51] The experience of being a migrant is documented in the symbolic representations of the Calvinist refugee communities: in the *peregrinus* figure and especially in the so-called *schepchen Godes*, the tiny ship of God and God's flock on the wide, perilous sea. Another representation is on the seal of the aforementioned Jan Lasky, with the ship of God entering the harbor and the circumscription "in portu navigo," here meaning: being a stranger in the world, I shall only find security and peace by entering the safe harbor of God and God's church.[52] This overwhelming sense of being a stranger and a migrant deeply shaped the outlook and culture of the refugees and of the societies—especially the Dutch one—based on that experience. And in this respect too, we can observe the dialectic of traditional and modern elements mentioned at the beginning of this chapter. The origin of the peregrine representation and outlook was not at all universalistic; rather, it was traditionally and existentially linked to an eschatological ideology that excluded other confessions—let alone non-Christian religions—and reserved dogmatic purity, truth, and eternal salvation for one's own group. In the long run, however, this traditional mentality of dogmatically exclusive peregrine status became secularized to a universalistic status for all migrants and strangers no matter their religion, race, or social status.

It can be assumed that the peregrine experience also influenced the attitude toward and the relationship with the complementary peregrine group: the Jews. It has even been argued that the Calvinist refugees represent a "third Reformation" with a specific refugee theology centered on the idea that all men are strangers and that this theology opened the minds and souls for a deeper understanding of the plight of the Jews.[53] But apart from these and other theological considerations (such as the thesis of a general connection between Christian chiliasm (millenarianism) and philo-Semitism[54] that must be evaluated by theologians, it seems quite clear that societies and cultures influenced by a refugee- and minority tradition developed quite different and more liberal attitudes toward strangers and minorities—and consequently also toward Jews—than those without this experience.

In this respect the confessional culture of Continental Lutherans (and, by the way, of Continental Catholics too) of central or eastern Europe, was quite different from the culture of the western European, "maritime" Calvinists. Apart from the small group of Gnesio or Flaccian[55] Lutherans— who, owing to the dogmatic schism after Luther's death also experienced exile, but never had the chance to influence the common Lutheran identity—German Lutheran political culture was based on stability of place and legal security under the protection of the Peace of Augsburg in 1555. Consequently, it was characterized by the territorialism of the *Landeskirchen* and by a parochialism that was concerned with the spiritual and social well-being of the autochthonous inhabitants and that tended to regard strangers as intruders and *Störenfriede* (troublemakers). This territorial and parochial culture of commitment to church and state as well as to social and cultural stability was an excellent basis for the rise of the well-ordered state and its responsibility for the well-being of its members—the predecessor of the *Sozialstaat* of the nineteenth and twentieth centuries. However, a peregrine mentality and its corresponding culture of understanding and empathy toward and acceptance of strangers could hardly flourish on this basis.[56] One could argue, with some plausibility, that it was less the respective teaching of Luther or Calvin in regard to Jews, but the different experience of migration and minority status during the confessional era that has been responsible for the different attitudes of the two Protestant confessional cultures toward Jews during early modern times. German Lutheran theologians, such as Dietrich Bonhoeffer, whose theological and intellectual profile was shaped by intensive exchange with and long visits to the western and southern European churches, were resistent to the Nazi ideology and its anti-Semitism. The Bishops of the Deutsche Christen (the Nazi branch of German Protestantism, and closely linked to their "Blut- und Boden" [blood and soil] ideology), on the other hand, declared that even "die christliche Taufe" could change nothing "an der rassischen Eigenart eines Juden, seiner Volkszugehörigkeit und seinem biologischen Sein"[57] (that even the Christian baptism would change nothing in the racial character of a Jew, of his ethnic origin and biological essence).

IV   The European Crisis of the
     Early Seventeenth Century and
     the Birth of an International
     State System

Religion and Early Modern State Power—
Preliminary Reflections

The impact of the Reformation and subsequent confessionalization and transcontinental migration, as we saw in chapter 3, was part of a much broader process of change in early modern social and political formation. Most influential was the alliance between confessionalization and early modern state building.[1] From the beginning, confessionalization research has been interested in the internal consequences of this alliance: the new personal, institutional, and bureaucratic capacities of the state; the incorporation of the national or territorial confessional churches; the control of morals, thinking and behavior, and so on.[2] Meanwhile these aspects are well researched and described in dozens of case studies.[3] In contrast to this, the complementary impact of confessionalization on the formation and rise of the modern international system of power states has engendered less interest among historians, even though it is quite obvious that the crisis in the relationships of the European states around 1600 was a religious as well as political one and that the ensuing wars were at the same time state wars and confessional wars.[4] In the following I shall try to overcome this neglect, arguing that this combination of religion and politics provided essential impulses for a fundamental change in the structure and functioning of international politics. The new organization and order of early modern state relations came to its ultimate breakthrough with the three peace treaties of the middle of the seventeenth century: the Peace of Westphalia, of the Pyrenees, and of Oliva, by which the transformation from medieval gradualism and universalism (with a pope and emperor at the top) toward the early modern secular and pluralistic state system was completed.

As we shall see, the experience of a close alliance (in some respect, even identity) of religion and politics, that the European states and societies underwent in the early modern period, could be of some relevance to the current world situation, when fundamentalism is posing a radical challenge to human conviviality within and between the states—not so much in official relations between states, but all the more strongly in informal relations. At present it might be of some interest to be reminded that Europe has had its own close experience with fundamentalist tendencies, resulting from the structural interference of religion and politics, of sacral and secular forces. And it might be helpful to analyze the instruments and paths by which European civilization was able to overcome the crisis and to establish permanent barriers against religious fundamentalism as a driving force in state relationships.

The height of confessionalization was generally associated with an unrestrained readiness for *total confrontation*, not merely for religious or ideological motives but also for social and political ones. Its fundamentalist qualities derived mainly from the fact that it was interpreted as an eschatological event, an apocalyptic struggle between the armies of Christ and Antichrist. With the wars of religion, or, to be more precise, the confessional wars of the late sixteenth and early seventeenth centuries, we are addressing a problem that, from the perspective of modern, "enlightened" Western society we would like to relegate to the "darkest" Middle Ages—had we not recently been most brutally reminded that a fundamentalist religious view of politics and the religious wars to which it gives rise are still real categories in international relations.[5]

Some preliminary remarks on method and approach seem in order. First, during the period under consideration, foreign policy and the international system were structurally different from the classical phase of European power politics during the nineteenth century, when the states, their diplomacy, and the law of nations were fully developed. In the early modern period, especially before 1650, the state was not yet fully formed and still had considerable weaknesses and drawbacks. The early modern states did not have a monopoly on foreign policy nor were all instruments of foreign policy (such as a diplomatic corps or central foreign offices) yet at its disposal. In consequence, non- or semi-state agents such as estates, the churches and their personnel, merchants, intellectuals, and even artists (such as the English poet Sir Philip Sidney and the Flemish painter Peter Paul Rubens) took part in international affairs. In this respect, international politics during the pre–nation state period of early modern Europe is comparable with similar structures in our increasingly post–nation state world. During the confessional period it was primarily the churches and their religious or ecclesiastical personnel that appeared as informal international agents, sometimes working in concordance with, sometimes in opposition to, the interests of the princes and the states.

Secondly, with regard to the periodization of early modern state relations I would distinguish four phases:

1. the period of Habsburg universalism and the challenge to it by France and the Ottoman Empire, beginning with the French King Charles VIII's invasion of Italy in 1494, and ending with the peace of Cateau-Cambrésis (1559);

2. the subsequent century (1559 to 1659/60) of Spanish hegemony and its challenge, by the Protestant sea powers Holland and England—and eventually, after the 1630s, by France under the superior leadership of Cardinal Richelieu;

3. the middle of the seventeenth century, followed by a period of international relations under the Westphalian Peace system, guaranteed by Sweden and France and ending with the Peace of Nystad of 1721;

4. the period of a fully functioning balance of power system under the pentarchy of the five great powers France, Britain, Russia, Austria, and Prussia, a pentarchy that ceased to be in force with the European wars bred by the French Revolution.

Third, I note the driving forces of early modern foreign politics, which also differed considerably from those of the nineteenth century, the most important being *dynasty* and its honor or reputation. Other forces include *religion* and its confessional dogmatism; *interest of states*, with regard to territorial expansion and also increasingly to economic opportunities; and finally, a more general factor that could be described as *traditional* or *long-term historical* constellations. The interplay among these driving forces and the change in dominance over time shaped the state relations of the early modern period decisively.[6]

The Crisis of the early Seventeenth Century

Defined in terms of leading factors, the century from 1550 to 1650, when Charles V's concept of a universal empire had failed and a new concept for international order beyond universalistic ideas was not yet at hand,[7] was a period of close alliance between political and confessional interest. On the one hand, the newly established Catholic bloc, led by Spain and the Habsburgs, in close alliance with the intellectual and moral power of the new, early modern Tridentine Catholicism, claimed hegemony on the basis of a reestablished religious and ecclesiastical—and that could not be other than Roman Catholic—uniformity in Europe. On the other hand, the Protestant powers, led first by the Netherlands and England, and later by the Rhine Palatinate, became threatened by the rising political as well as intellectual and moral power of this confessionalized Catholicism—the more so as the Saint Bartholomew's Eve massacre, the Spanish Armada, and the legal and political offensive in Germany awakened a sense of immanent danger. Alarmed by these developments, a determined group of Protestant princes and politicians, mainly of the Reformed or Calvinist branch, was eager to resist and oppose the Catholics *à tout prix*. In this constellation, religion and confession also became leading factors in international relations and the interpretation of world affairs, as the eschatological battle between the forces of Christ and Antichrist, common in Christian thinking, became more and more frequent. Of course, it goes without saying that religion never dominated the foreign policy of the European powers absolutely; rather, it functioned together with other forces, among which the previously mentioned key forces were the most important of a kind of syndrome. During the decades around 1600, however, religion and confession became, for approximately one generation, the most dynamic and powerful factor within this syndrome.

Consequently, the crisis of the decades around 1600 and the subsequent long period of wars arose from a combination of religious, political, and cultural processes. The political constellation, which can be touched on only briefly here,[8] was characterized by the rivalries among the European dynasties and by the increasing competition within the rising system of states about political, economical, cultural and other secular interests. In the 1590s, nearly all regions of Europe (and its colonies) experienced growing tension and rivalry between rising and declining states: in western and southern Europe between Spain and the northwestern sea powers of the Dutch Republic and England. France and the Turks, the great counterparts of Spain during the first half of the century, were pushed into the background: France, because of its internal problems; the Turks, because they had retreated from the western parts of the Mediterranean Sea and in the early 1580s had accepted peace with Spain. A similar competition was at hand in central Europe. The Holy Roman Empire experienced a fierce confrontation over political, fiscal, cultural and, last but not least, military competence between the emperor and the estates together with conflicts between the territorial princes themselves: to the southeast, in Hungary, Transylvania, and the Danubian Principalities, a sometimes hot, sometimes cold war took place among the Habsburgs, the Turks (during the so-called *Langen Türkenkrieg* [Long Turkish War], 1593–1606) and regional princes such as the Báthory, Bocskay, Aron Tyranul of Walachia, and the famous Mihai Vietazul (Michael the Brave) of Moldavia (1593–1601). Simultaneously, in the Baltic-Scandinavian region a long-term struggle was fought among the traditional powers of Denmark and Poland, the rising powers of Sweden and Russia, and the once powerful, but now declining agents such as the Hanseatic League and the small bishoprics of Livonia.

These secular conflicts notwithstanding, it is obvious that within the syndrome of forces responsible for the development of international affairs at that time, the confes-

sional factor, which linked politics to dogmatic and ecclesiological positions of the confessional churches, gained more
and more prominence from the 1580s onward. The correla-
tion of religious and political forces in international affairs
had already been analyzed in the early sixteenth century by
Erasmus. In his *Querela Pacis* he observes that (1) "Angulus
hostis est Gallo, nec ob aliud nisi quod Gallus est"[9] (the Eng-
lishman is hostile to the Frenchman with no other reason
than that he is a Frenchman); and (2) that both the French
and the English (as well as the Spaniards and the Germans)
rely on Christian symbols when waging war against each
other: "vexilla crucem habeant; pugnat crux cum cruce,
Christus adversus Christum belligertur"[10] (their flags have
the cross as sign; cross fights against cross, Christ against
Christ). Erasmus still had the vision that these were only
family conflicts, which should be settled by a revival of the
populus christianus idea. In reality, the protonational sentiments together with the military claim of religious symbols
were an expression of irreversible differentiation and par-
ticularization. And as Reformation and confessionalization
widened the religious and ecclesiastical differences, religion
and confession became an essential part of the cultural and
political identity of the early modern states and nations.
During the second decade of the seventeenth century, confession became a dominant and key force in foreign policy,
not only with regard to the symbols mentioned by Erasmus,
but also with regard to political identity and ideology, the
style of politics, cultural representation of the princes and
the states, as well as the questions of alliances, legitimation,
and propaganda. Such dominance was obvious in the internal German power struggle with the founding of the Protestant Union in May 1608 and the Catholic League a good year
later; it was even visible to a degree in France. As the great

Cardinal and Prime Minister Richelieu himself repeatedly and plausibly claimed, France, despite its real alliances with Protestant powers, would have liked nothing better than to orientate its foreign policy by confessional, Catholic considerations. But, the great cardinal and foreign politician explained, such was not possible because Spain had split international Catholicism and was conducting anti-French hegemonic policy under the pretext of religion.

This advancement of confessional factors was to become one of the leading forces (*Leitkräfte*) in the internal relations between the European rulers and the rising power states and was the last step in confessionalization. In parallel with the formation of the churches and of society internally, relations between the states were confessionalized as well. As early as 1565 in France, a member of the Guise party alerted the king to the new key function of religion or confession in foreign affairs: "These days the Catholic princes may not act as they did earlier. In those days, friend and foe were divided by the borders and territories of the kingdoms. . . . Today that must be: Catholic and heretic, and a Catholic prince must have all the Catholics in all states as his friends, just as the heretic prince must have all heretics as his friends and vassals, regardless of whether they are his own vassals or the vassals of others." And in 1578 the Hessian landgrave Wilhelm, who was by no means one of the most extreme confessionalists of his age, called religion the "härteste vinculum . . . stabiliendi foederis"[11] (the hardest and most stabile basis for alliances between rulers and states). As a consequence of this connection between religion and politics, for a number of years, confessional conflicts and wars of religion were endemic in Europe, both within states and between individual territories and societies. And contrary to the maxim of sovereignty and to the principles of modern international law, which were only just developing, intervention on confessional reasons became commonplace in foreign policy: "Catholic and Protestant princes must have friends among Catholics and Protestants respectively regardless of whether they are his own vassals or the vassals of others!"

The confessional semantics spread rapidly. In addition to the confessional shaping the horizon of political action and concepts among the political and cultural elite, the confessional pattern of interpreting international affairs was promulgated extensively by pamphlets and propaganda; by theological treatises, hymns, and chorales; by reports of diplomats and lawyers; and even in the correspondence of private and public persons. Parallel to the political and psychological crisis that developed within and between European societies at the end of the century, this confessional interpretation gained prophetic and partly apocalyptic features, by which political and military events or diplomatic initiatives and alliances between the European rulers and power blocs were evaluated in an eschatological perspective. This perspective was common to all three confessional cultures, though in different representations. Catholicism "tended to see itself in the tradition of a single, undivided Christianity and consequently presented the struggle against confessional opponents primarily as a fight against the heretical threat to *Christianitas*," presented mainly in crusading metaphors, or as fight against a diabolic illness: the *pestis Germaniae*. In contrast, Protestants preferred the apocalyptic pattern: the Calvinists, aggressively and politically; the Lutherans in a more psychological, self-reflective way, blaming themselves and their sinful life for God's just wrath and all secular disaster it sent upon them.[12]

.   .   .

The offensive and aggressive character of Calvinism obviously stemmed from the fact that Calvinism was directly confronted by the Catholic religious, legal, diplomatic, and military offensive: in Geneva, France, the Netherlands, northwestern Germany, and to some extent, even in Britain. Lutheranism, by contrast, generally enjoyed legal protection—as in the Holy Roman Empire or in Scandinavia. In the face of this threat and psychologically startled by the experience of the Saint Bartholomew's Eve massacre of 1572 in Paris, the Spanish Fury of 1576 at Antwerp, and the threat of the Spanish Armada in 1588, Calvinism developed a radical, confessional propaganda in the form of pamphlets that interpreted contemporary events in general and those in the international system in particular in eschatological terms of the history of religious salvation. The origins of this specifically Calvinist view of history are to be found among the circle of refugee churches (described in chapter 3). No less a figure than Philip Marnix van Sint Aldegonde (1540–98), close counselor of Wilhelm of Orange and author of the Wilhelmus national hymn of the Netherlands, devoted himself to working for the rapid dissemination of the religious-biblical interpretation of contemporary history: the people of the Netherlands, and a little later, the English too, were to see themselves as God's chosen people. Their struggle against the Spaniards was the struggle of the Israelites against Pharaoh and the Egyptians. William of Orange was "onse Moyses," or else David in his fight against the tyrant Saul. In the "Wilhelmus-hymn," William of Orange was celebrated in the form of David's psalmody, and perhaps the most concise expression of Marnix's historical theology can be found in the preface to the second edition of his translation of the psalms.[13]

From the perspective of these political-theological semantics, the tension of the political crises and the military
conflicts it obviously bred were nothing less than the eschatological struggle between Christ and Antichrist, between
the forces of good and evil, between the children of light
and of darkness, as prophesied in the Book of Revelation of
the New Testament. In combination with political activism,
typical for many rulers and their counselors at that time,
this eschatological interpretation resulted in a widespread
perspective that I term *confessional fundamentalism.* This
perspective was characterized by two main features: its un-
shakable self-assurance that one was definitely on the side
of the angels; and its activism, stemming from the convic-
tion that salvation was at stake and that consequently the
children of God in this last battle had to fight Antichrist
by all means, whatever the secular costs. Such an eschatological thinking was even common within the diplomatic
world, as can be seen by the official correspondence of Pieter Cornelisz. Brederode, envoy from the Estates-General
of the Netherlands to the West German Protestant Imperial Estates. His writing is shaped by a "decidedly confes-
sionalist perception of power relations and lines of conflict
in Europe." Brederode "constantly pushed confession to the
center" of his negotiations.[14] His aim was to confront international Catholicism, which the Protestant princes and
states were increasingly experiencing as a threat to their existence. To cope with this danger, he emphatically called
for a Protestant counteralliance, one that would include all
Protestant countries—the Netherlands, the Protestant Imperial Estates, England, Denmark, and Sweden—and one
to whom the pope and Spain would be "Antichrist ende vi-
andt" (Antichrist and common enemy).[15]

From Confrontation to Compromise and Peace— Overcoming Confessional Fundamentalism

This Christian fundamentalism resulted in and led to the chaos of the longest and most dreadful war of religion and states Europe ever experienced. In the end, however, it also led to the development of totally new legal and intellectual instruments and concepts to overcome the crisis and to avoid the fundamentalist trap. It is disputable whether the outbreak of the war really was inevitable. In fact, the actors were aware of the dangers of fundamentalist policy: if the Bohemian Estates elect Frederick of the Palatinate (the head of the aggressive Calvinistic internationalism movement) for their king, warned Ferdinand of Wittelsbach, elector and archbishop of Cologne, brother of Duke Maximilian of Bavaria, and one of the leaders of the Catholic bloc on the eve of war, "then they might as well prepare for a twenty, thirty, or even forty years' war."[16] In order to prevent this, Elector Frederick V of the Palatinate and his antipode in the Catholic camp, the Bavarian Duke Maximilian, negotiated to the last.[17] And in complement to the war-mongering propaganda of the confessional blocs, peace pamphlets by irenic and humanistic circles referred to the piety of the simple religious person in order to admonish politicians and theologians to overcome their ideological differences. The most prominent of these pamphlets and well known even today is the pamphlet *Geistlicher Rauffhandel*, contrasting the peace-loving Christian (presented as a simple shepherd) with the belligerent church leaders.[18] Even plans for a superconfessional European peace system were developed; for example, in 1581 by the humanist Heinrich Rantzau, councillor to the king of Denmark.[19] Yet, and this makes the situation even more gloomy, neither fear of the foreseeable chaos nor the various strategies for avoiding war were able to stop the fundamentalist dynamics of confrontation.

The events are well known and need only to be recalled: the outbreak of the impending military conflict in 1618 in Bohemia and the triumphant victory of the Catholic army in the 1620 Battle of the White Mountain under an icon of Holy Mary and with the battle cry "Sancta Maria"; the extension of the conflagration to the empire as a whole; the triumphant progress of the Catholic and imperial forces as far as the shore of the Baltic Sea with the famously unsuccessful siege of Stralsund by Wallenstein; the Edict of Restitution of 1629 as an apogee that, if it had been implemented, would have given permanent supremacy to Catholicism and the Catholic states in Germany and consequently would have changed decisively the confessional balance in Europe in favor of Catholicism; the Peace of Lübeck with Denmark in the same year; then the change in fortunes in favor of the Protestants by Sweden's intervention; finally, France's entry into the war in 1635 and the shift in emphasis from a war of religion to a political war of states that during the last decade turned into an unprecedented brutalization.[20] In the end, however, there were the three peace treaties, mentioned at the outset, by which war was not eliminated but tamed and—a striking German expression—*eingehegt* (enclosed). For the rest of the early modern period, war was bound to rational considerations, rendering a fundamentalist short circuit (as in the early seventeenth century) unlikely.

This successful turn from a policy of confrontation and war to a policy of compromise and peace[21] raises two highly topical questions. First, how did Europe extricate itself from the chaos of fundamentalist confrontation, which at its height had called the very basis of Latin European civilization and the possibility of human conviviality into question? Second, what legal and institutional precautions were taken to make sure that fundamentalism was permanently overcome and that relations between states would be placed on a rational and secular—that is, on a modern autonomous—basis?

In the chaos of external and internal wars between the confessions and their power blocs it became clear that a new internal stability and secure external peace could be achieved only by a paradigmatic shift in the structure and concept of politics. That Europe, despite the deep political antagonism and fundamentalist ideological hostility by which it was disunited for more than a generation, was ripe for such a radical change in the maxims and principles of its social and political organization was essentially owed to two pillars of the Latin type of civilization: law and religion. In the tradition of Roman law, the law had shaped the civilization of Latin Europe deeply from the very beginning. In the early modern period it became a decisive instrument to organize the balance of power within the rising states as well as their external relations: by natural law, the law of the people, the law of war (discussed by a wide variety of theologians and lawyers and most recently compiled by Hugo de Groot), and last but not least, by the principle of sovereignty and autonomy of the secular power, developed in the midst of the chaos of civil and religious war by Bodin and the Politiques in France and by Thomas Hobbes in England. In this perspective it was the tradition of Roman law and rational and pragmatic political theory that had produced the preconditions for the ultimate success of peace negotiations and in the long run, the new system of "Droit public de l'Europe," which, based on European ideals and institutions, became the instrument of global organization of the relations between the modern states.[22] But it is doubtful that fundamentalism could have been defeated permanently, without a complementary tradition of peace, rooted in *religion* and the specific religious and ecclesiastical settlements of Latin Europe.

Given the fundamentalist tendencies and the enormous potential for confessional conflict, the Westphalian Peace Congress would probably have never succeeded in overcoming the crisis of enforcing the new principles had Europe's capacity for peace not been anchored also in *religion* itself. Indisputably, religion contributed in Latin Europe to violence and wars, not least because the Roman church itself had built up a state and thus become a state agent in the system of powers. Nonetheless, the capacity of religion to foster peace is equally obvious. It was based essentially on the already described dualistic structures of the church-state settlement, which made the sacral and the secular, the ecclesiastical and secular order always distinguishable. Under these conditions, neither religion or churchmen nor politics or politician could ever unconditionally subjugate the other to its norms, as in the case of monistic systems. In principle this situation remained in force even during the apogee of confessionalism, when fundamentalist tendencies challenged this settlement. And this situation raised at least five implications for the character of the Thirty Years' War and the conditions for permanently settling the crisis.

First, as the example of Catholic France shows, politics always remained independent enough of expansive confessionalization to be able to act against confessional and religious interests, even if these acts were always a temporary exception to the rule. Second, even when the princes and magistrates—as *defensores ecclesiae* (defenders of the Faith), as in the case of Catholic territories, or *Notbischöfe* (emergency bishops) or *praecipua membra ecclesiae* (outstanding members of the church), in the case of Protestant ones—put their political actions into the service of their respective confession, they remained committed to both parts of their office: to religious care for their subjects with regard to their eternal salvation, and to secular care with regard to their well-being in this world (*Fürsorge für die Untertanen*). And if the commitment in one field was fatal for the duties in the other field, the terms of that commitment had to be changed. Even at the high point of confessionalism, Europe was not dominated by a fundamentalist monism for which religion was the only and ultimate norm. When the war made it obvious that too close an alliance between politics and religion would ruin not only the state and society, but ultimately also the churches and religion, it was the dualistic constitution of Latin Christianity that offered the ability and crucial legitimation for a thoroughgoing revision of political confessionalism. On this basis, the eagerness to go to war, which during the first third of the century had dominated the princes and magistrates as well as theologians and churchmen, could become the opposite and turn, during the late 1630s, into a widespread willingness for peace.

Third, the solution of 1648 that resulted from this readiness for peace, and that precluded a future European war of religion of the type of the Thirty Years' War, was made possible by the fact that a tendency toward secularization was inherent in Europe's dualistic religious constitution; that is, a tendency toward separating secular and religious matters and toward autonomous self-determination in politics, culture, and society. This secular process, with roots deep in the Middle Ages, was not totally blocked, even at the high point of confessionalism, but continued in the form of an undercurrent—in particular, in the theoretical and practical strategies for solutions pursued by lawyers and political thinkers in general. These strategies helped smooth the path toward peace.

Fourth and, perhaps even more important, secularization conferred on the policy of peace pursued by the Catholic and Protestant princes a particular *legitimacy* without which the confessional fundamentalism could not have been overcome so quickly. For, as I argued in chapter 2, until the Enlightenment, secularization was not predominantly an antireligious or anticlerical movement, but was closely associated with religious-ecclesiastical traditions. The end of monasticism in Old Europe was characterized by a dialectic that did not halt the religious dynamic, but absorbed it into the worldly sphere and thus crucially strengthened the effectiveness and the legitimacy of political and social actions and settlements—as can be demonstrated by the symbolic representation of peace by the *dove of peace*, a religious as well as secular symbol. As alreday mentioned in chapter 2, the dove carrying an olive twig in its beak was the Old Testament's bird of peace, which showed Noah that the earth was habitable again after the raging of the elements, and showed also that God had reconciled himself with humans, again, and was offering them his peace. And the Peace of Westphalia consequently was understood as secular as well as religious or sacred peace: "pax sit Christiana."[23]

Fifth, the most important and far-reaching consequences of secularization are the modern autonomy of politics and consequently the strict prohibition against military intervention for religious reasons. Today, hardly anything evokes broader agreement in Europe than the rejection of religious war and everyone is deeply concerned about remnants or elements of religious wars—as in the conflicts in Northern Ireland and in the Balkans, and especially in regard to fundamentalist terror. After the paradigmatic shift of the mid-seventeenth century in the understanding of religion and politics and of the ways in which they may cooperate, the confessional theory of legal intervention—"a Catholic prince must have all the Catholics in all states as his friends, just as the heretic prince must have all heretics as his friends and vassals, regardless of whether they are his own vassals or the vassals of others"—this principle that opened the door for intervention for religious reason, was no longer valid (see page 74). Instead, a statement of Hugo Grotius became the ultimate maxim for internal as well as external relations between men and states—"Paci Christianorum studentis officium et hoc est, demoliri dogmata, quae pacem civilem perturbant. Prius est, bonum civem esse, quam bonum Christianum"[24] (Peace among Christians is only possible if the dogmas are given up, that intervene with the political peace)—though Grotius was wrong in his assumption that people had to choose either to be "good Christians" or "good citizens." The decisive progress of the new settlement was that men could be both: good Christians *and* good citizens.

Here, I think, is one of the positive messages of my story: theoretically as well as historically it is possible to separate religion and politics without doing harm or injustice to either. On this basis it should be possible to overcome present-day fundamentalism as well, giving all people the understanding that religious truth and salvation do not enter into the peaceful resolution of secular matters. Religious righteousness and orthodoxy do not exclude, but rather they *include* the obligation to be a "good and peaceful citizen."

The New Stability of a Secular Order of Autonomous States

In conclusion, some reflections on the preconditions and the structure of the newly established Early Modern system of European power states seem in order. Undoubtedly the sepa-

ration of state and church, religion and politics by the peace
system of the middle of the seventeenth century marked a
turning point in European as well as in world history. That
makes it more important to describe and understand the
role and function of religion within the process of coupling
and separating confessional and secular matters from the
end of the sixteenth to the middle of the seventeenth centuries. After our analysis, it seems obvious that it would be
misleading to assess the apogee of confessionalism in the
decades around 1600—its penchant for fundamentalist tendencies notwithstanding—as a period of backwardness or
even regression. We should not regard European confessionalization in general as a brake on social change. On the contrary, a historical analysis that looks for the structures and
functions of religion in this time of early modern formation
shows that the focus on confessional religion gave way to
the dynamization and modernization of the European societies—to use a controversial term to describe a highly differentiated phenomenon.

Confessionalization and the European Christian fundamentalism it had fostered around 1600 was overcome fifty
years later, not by going against religion, or by abolishing
or ignoring it, but by going with religion. Indeed, the solution came out of religion. I have attributed this result to the
specific religious-sociological structures of Latin Christian
Europe. Whether something similar could be said of other
world religions and their world civilizations needs to be the
subject of further research. We should be careful not to make
quick equations; for example, if the media today speak of
confessions with regard to the Shiites. Everything that I have
read about the various groupings within Islam suggests that
they are *not* the equivalents of the confessional ideological
systems of the early modern period in Europe, which were

dogmatic and precisely defined, extremely homogeneous as a result of a high degree of internal integration, and clearly exclusive toward the outside. Yet this, too, is just a first hypothesis that needs to be tested in detail.

By the mid-seventeenth century, Europe had reached in its secular order and state relationships a turning point. Not in the sense that it had established the "eternal peace"—the French *Roi Soleil* as early as the 1660s had started a new series of European wars. The newfound political stability was the stability of the age of courts and alliances,[25] characterized by rational (and consequently nonfundamentalist) institutions and principles: the autonomy of politics; the legal equality of the states and their right to conduct their henceforth exclusively secular interests of state. Consequently there was a free play of alliances between these secular and autonomous actors in the international system, now appearing unequivocally and exclusively as states.

In this system, war remained a legitimate means of state policy, but no longer of the unrestrained, fundamentalist kind seen in the total confrontation of the Thirty Years' War and its struggle of religious ideologies. It was the age of alliance wars and cabinet wars that used military means in a rational and calculated way. From the very start, these wars were conducted with the clear goal of a new peace and the readjustment of the European system of powers. A new phase of total ideological confrontation and fundamentalistic wars between European powers arose only one-and-a-half centuries later with the Wars of the French Revolution. Conducted under the banner of modern nationalism, this can be seen as a secular variant of Early Modern confessionalism.

Notes

I. Introduction

1. See Peter Burke, "Did Europe Exist before 1700?" *History of European Ideas* 1 (1980): 1–29. For later periods: Hartmut Kaelble, *Europäer über Europa: Die Entstehung des europäischen Selbstverständnisses im 19. und 20. Jahrhundert* (Frankfurt am Main: Campus, 2001).

2. See Marc Bloch, *Mélanges historiques* (Paris: SEVPEN: 1963), 16–40.

3. It is not possible to cite here all relevant research projects and publications. For modern social history, see Hartmut Kaelble, "Comparative European Social History," in *Encyclopedia of European Social History from 1350 to 2000*, ed. Peter N. Stearns (New York: Scribner, 2001), 1:113–121, and its extensive bibliography. For an explicitly European comparative approach to early modern ecclesiastical, cultural, and political history, see the following on confessionalization: Joel F. Harrington and Helmut Walser Smith, "Confessionalization, Community, and State Building in Germany, 1555–1870," *Journal of Modern History* 69 (1997): 77–101; Ute Lotz-Heumann, "The concept of 'confessionalization': Historiographical paradigm in dispute," *Memoria y Civilizatións* 4 (2001): 93–114; Stefan Ehrenpreis and Ute Lotz-Heumann, *Reformation und konfessionelles Zeitalter* (Darmstadt: Wissenschaftliche Buchgesellschaft, 2002); Focal point: "Confessionalization and Social Discipline in France, Italy, and Spain," *Archiv für Reformationsgeschichte / Archive for Reformation History* 94 (2003): 276–319; Heinz Schilling, "Confessionalization: Historical and Scholarly Perspectives of a Comparative and Interdisciplinary

Paradigm," in John M. Headley et al., eds., *Confessionalization in Europe, 1555–1700. Essays in Honour and Memory of Bodo Nischan* (Aldershot: Ashgate, 2004), 21–35; Heinz Schilling and István Tóth, *Religion and Cultural Exchange* (see below, note 6). See also chapter 2.

4. Especially impressive (because written by a single author) is the Italian masterpiece by Giuseppe Galasso, *Storia d'Europa*: vol. 1, *Antichità e Medioevo*; vol. 2, *Età Moderna*; vol. 3, *Età Contemporanea* (Rome: Laterza, 1996). A lavish compilation of works by leading European historians is *Europa: The European Idea and Identity, from Ancient Greece to the 21st Century*, ed. Eric Bussière et al. (Antwerp: Mercatorfonds, 2001). On contemporary development, see Tony Judt, *Postwar: A History of Europe since 1945* (New York: Penguin, 2005). See also the four-volume European history series *Siedler Geschichte Europas*: Hagen Schulze, *Phönix Europa. Die Moderne. Von 1750 bis heute*; Heinz Schilling, *Die neue Zeit. Vom Christenheitseuropa zum Europa der Staaten, 1250–1750*; Michael Borgolte, *Christen, Juden, Muselmanen. Die Erben der Antike und der Aufstieg des Abendlandes, 300–1400*; and Christian Meier, *Die Alte Welt. Griechische Pollis, römisches Imperium, Entstehung des Christentums* (Berlin: Siedler, 1998, 1999, 2006, and 2008). See also Peter Blickle, ed., *Handbuch der Geschichte Europas*, 10 vols. (Stuttgart: Eugen Ulmer, 2001ff.). An exhibition of particular relevance is that organized by Marie-Louise von Plessen: "Idee Europa. Entwürfe zum 'Ewigen Frieden'" (2003) for the Deutsches Historisches Museum at Berlin and later displayed in Brussels.

5. Wim Blockmans and Jean-Philippe Genet, eds., *The Origins of the Modern State in Europe*, 7 vols. (Oxford: Oxford University Press, 1995ff.). In the last decade of the twentieth century the Dutch endowment for scientific research financed the priority program "The Netherlands Culture in European Context," with four volumes organized on four periodical focus points: vol. 1, *1650: Bevochten eenndracht*; vol. 2, *1800: Blauwdrukken voor een samenleving*; vol. 3, *1900: Hoogtij van een burgerlijke cultuur*; vol. 4, *1950: Welvaart in zwart-wit* (The Hague: SDU Uitgevers, 1999).

6. Bernhard Jussen, ed., *Die Macht des Königs. Herrschaft in Europa vom Frühmittelalter bis in die Neuzeit* (München: C. H. Beck,

2005); the four volumes of the European Science Foundation program *Cultural Exchange in Europe, 1400–1700*: vol. I, Heinz Schilling and István Tóth, eds., *Religion and Cultural Exchange, 1400–1700*; vol. 2, Donatella Calabi and Turk Christensen, eds., *Cities and Cultural Exchange in Europe, 1400–1700*; vol. 3, Francisco Bethencourt and Florike Egmond, eds., *Correspondence and Cultural Exchange in Europe, 1400–1700*; vol. 4, Herman Roodenburg, ed., *Forging European Identities, 1400–1700* (Cambridge: Cambridge University Press, 2007). For a similar approach, see Pieter Roodenburg and Pieter Spierenburg, eds., *Social Control in Europe, 1500–1800* (Columbus: Ohio State University Press, 2004), and Simonetta Cavaciocchi, ed., *Le migrazioni in Europa, secc. XIII–XVIII* (Florence: Le Monnier, 1994).

7. This idea is extensively discussed with reference to similar development in other European countries and in the Netherlands in "De Arena. Debat over zin af onzin van een nationale canon," *Bijdragen en Mededelingen betreffende de Geschiedenis der Nederlanden* 121 (2006), 76–105; the articles included are E. Jonker's "Op eieren lopen. Canonvorming met een slecht geweten" (76–92), and James K. Kennedy's "The Dutch Canon Debate. Reflections of an American" (99–105).

8. See the essay on these programmatic developments as viewed by the doyen of "Gesellschaftsgeschichte" in Germany, Hans-Ulrich Wehler: Wehler, "Transnationale Geschichte—der neue Königsweg historischer Forschung?" in Gunilla Budde et al., eds., *Transnationale Geschichte. Themen, Tendenzen und Theorien* (Göttingen: Vandenhoeck Ruprecht, 2006), 161–174, with the conclusion

Im Ansatz der Transnationalen Geschichte steckt allzu leicht eine systematische Unterschätzung des *National*staats als lebensgeschichtlichem Bezugsrahmen und Loyalitätspol, im Zeichen des virulenten Nationalismus sogar als letztverbindliche Sinngebungsinstanz. . . . Wie die Globalisierungswellen sich auch verstärken mögen, auf absehbare Zeit bleiben die Nationalgesellschaften für viele Prozesse der entscheidende Rahmen. Es geht dabei nicht nur um das Verfassungsgerüst der modernen Nationalstaaten, sondern um einen entscheidenden gesellschaftlichen und kulturellen Handlungsraum, der sich nicht zuletzt durch die anhaltende nationalgeschichtliche Deutung der Vergangenheit immer wieder neu konstituiert und verstärkt. Die deutsche Neuzeitgeschichte bietet dafür ein anschauliches Beispiel. (173).

9. Thus the title of an influential book of Peter Laslett, *The World We Have Lost* (London: Methuen, 1965; 2nd ed., 1971).

10. John E. Wills, Jr., *1688 — A Global History* (New York: Norton, 2001).

11. Herman van der Wee, "Globalization. Core and Periphery in the World Economy of the Late Middle Ages and Early Modern Times," forthcoming in *Festschrift for Istvan Berend* (Toronto: University of Toronto Press, 2007).

12. See the introduction to my *Neue Zeit* (note 4). Wehler contradicts himself: on the one hand, he stresses the indisputable need for national categories for early modern and modern history of Europe (*Transnationale Geschichte*, 173); on the other hand, he criticizes the new collection in European history for paying too much attention to these national histories (Wehler, "Synthesekonzepte heute," in *Was ist der Mensch, was Geschichte? Jörn Rüsen zum 65. Geburtstag*, ed. Friedrich Jaeger and Jürgen Straub [Bielefeld: Transcript, 2005], 233–240, here 235). In my opinion, it is inevitable that we must give credit both to the different national histories *and* to the common features in the history of European civilization.

13. This idea and its methodological and theoretical implications are developed in more detail in the lecture I delivered in the Academiegebouw Universiteit Leiden in September 2002, the year I was Heineken Prize laureatus for European History. See Heinz Schilling, "Was heißt und zu welchem Ende studiert man europäisch vergleichende Geschichte?" in *Heineken Lectures 2002*, ed. Royal Netherlands Academy of Arts and Sciences (Amsterdam, 2002), 63–82. Meanwhile similar but philosophically and theoretically more elaborate ideas are developed in Jörn Rüsen, "Historical Consciousness. Narrative Structure, Moral Function and Ontogenetic Development," in *Theorizing Historical Consciousness*, ed. P. Seixas (Toronto: University of Toronto Press, 2004), 63–85, where "the otherness of different cultures" is identified "as a mirror that enables us to get a better self-understanding" (69). In the following that mirror is used in a macrohistorical manner to enable

European civilization to get a better understanding of its history in the perspective of global history.

14. In this respect as well, the Dutch scientific community reacted especially quickly to the radical change in the intellectual climate after 9/11 and a series of similar blows in the Netherlands itself. Within the national program "Cultural Reorientation and the Fundamental Principles of the Humanities," Ed Jonker from Utrecht University prepared the analysis "End of Postmodernism in the Humanities"; its end arises from the demand for "precise scientific reasons for judgements" even in the humanities (wetenschappelijke hardheid waarmee de oordelen ondersteund kunnen worden). See Jonker, "Canonvorming," (note 7 above) 77 n. 2.

15. See the convincing analysis of Gottfried Schramm's "Drei Schöpfer nationaler Alphabete für den Nordostrand der Christenheit (im 5., 9. und 15. Jahrhundert)," in *Universalgeschichte und Nationalgeschichte*, ed. Gangolf Hübinger und Jürgen Osterhammel, (Freiburg: Rombach, 1994), 73–103; Schramm, *Slawisch im Gottesdienst. Kirchenwortschatz und neue Schriftsprachen auf dem Weg zu einem christlichen Südosteuropa* (München: Oldenbourg, 2007).

16. Wolfgang Reinhard, "Die lateinische Variante von Religion für die politische Kultur Europas. Ein Versuch in historischer Anthropologie," *Saeculum* 43 (1992): 231–255. See Dietrich Gerhard, *Das Abendland 800 bis 1800. Ursprung und Gegenbild unserer Zeit* (Freiburg: Ploetz, 1985); Schilling, *Neue Zeit*; Schilling, "Was heißt."

17. Recent works that focus on these borderlands and the process of diffusion are Eszter Andor and István György Tóth, eds., *Frontiers of Faith. Religious Exchange and the Constitution of Religious Identities, 1400–1750* (Budapest: CEU/ESF, 2001); and Jerzy Kłoczowski, "L'expérience de pluralisme religieux et culturel des ruthènes," in *Il Battesimo delle Terre Russe. Bilancio di un Milennio*, ed. S. Graciotti (Florence: Casa Editrice Leo S. Orschki, 1991), 303–322. On the East European Uniate Church, see Oskar Halcki, *From Florence to Brest, 1439–1596* (Rome: Sacrum Poloniae Millenium, 1958); Ernst Christoph Suttner, "Unionsabschlüsse östlicher Kirchen mit der Kirche von Rom im 16. und 17. Jahrhundert," *Ostkirchliche Studien* 46 (1997): 227–247; H. Litwin, "Catholicization

among the Ruthenian Nobility and Assimilating Processes in the Ukraine during the years 1589–1648," *Acta Poloniae Historiae* 55 (1987): 57–83. On the church's present-day situation, see Hans-Dieter Döpmann, "Zur Problematik des erneuerten Uniatismus," in *Kirche und Gläubige im postsowjetischen Osteuropa*, ed. Werner Kosack (München: Beck, 1996) 53–73. See also Serhii Plokhy, *The Cossacks and Religion in Early Modern Ukraine* (Oxford: University Press, 2001).

18. For Reinhard Koselleck's concept of "Sattelzeit der Moderne," see the introduction to *Geschichtliche Grundbegriffe. Historisches Lexikon zur politisch-sozialen Sprache in Deutschland*, ed. Otto Brunner, Werner Konze, and Reinhard Koselleck, 8 vols. (Stuttgart: Klett, 1972–1993); 1:xiii–xxvii; Koselleck, *Futures past: On the Semantics of Historical Time*, trans. Keith Tribe (Cambridge, Mass.: MIT Press, 1985; New York: Columbia University Press, 2004); Koselleck, *The Practice of Conceptual History: Timing History, Spacing Concepts*, trans. Todd Samuel Presner et al., with a foreword by Hayden White (Stanford: Stanford University Press, 2002). See also Koselleck's posthumous collection, *Begriffsgeschichte. Studien zur Semantik und Pragmatik der politischen und sozialen Sprache* (Frankfurt am Main: Suhrkamp, 2006). On the reception of "Begriffsgeschichte" and Koselleck's thinking in general within the Anglo-Saxon world, see Hartmut Lehmann and Malvin Richter, eds., *The Meaning of Historical Terms and Concepts. New Studies on "Begriffsgeschichte"* (Washington, D.C.: Occasional Papers of the German Historical Institute, 1996), 15. On the concept of early modern "Vorsattelzeit," see Heinz Schilling, *Aufbruch und Krise. Deutsche Geschichte von 1517 bis 1648* (Berlin: Siedler, 1988), 313–370.

19. Schilling's, "Was heißt" offers more detail.

II. The Confessionalization of European Churches and Societies

1. The topics covered within this book qualify for "endless" annotation. To keep the notes under control I shall refer often to older publications of mine with extensive bibliographical notes. I

ask for your understanding regarding this measure of self-reference. For the medieval preconditions, see Hans Maier, "Am König bilden sich zwei Zapfen. Mythos und Symbol Canossa: Der kalte Krieg von Kaisermacht und Papsttum führte die Trennung von Kirche und Staat herauf," *Frankfurter Allgemeine Zeitung*, no. 89 (April 15, 2006): 39. For general considerations of law and constitutional development, see Ernst Wolfgang Böckenförde, "Die Entstehung des Staates als Vorgang der Säkularisation," in idem, ed., *Staat, Gesellschaft, Freiheit: Studien zur Staatstheorie und zum Verfassungsrecht* (Frankfurt am Main: Suhrkamp, 1976), 42–64; Heinz Schilling, "Der religionssoziologische Typus Europa als Bezugspunkt inner- und interzivilisatorischer Gesellschaftsvergleiche," in *Gesellschaften im Vergleich*, ed. Hartmut Kaelble and Jürgen Schriewer (Frankfurt am Main: Lang, 1998), 41–52.

2. The following position is developed in more detail and with substantial annotation in Heinz Schilling, "Riforma e affermazione delle chiese nazionali," in *Il Cristianesimo. Grande Atlante*, ed. Giuseppe Alberigo, Giuseppe Ruggieri, and Roberto Rusconi, vol 1, *Delle origini alle chiese contemporanee* (Turin: UTET, 2006), 184–202; idem, "The Europe of Churches and Confessions," in *Europa: The European Idea and Identity, from Ancient Greece to the 21st Century*, ed. Eric Bussière, Michel Dumoulin, and Gilbert Trausch (Antwerp: Mercatorfonds, 2001), 79–108; idem, *Die neue Zeit* (see above, chapter 1, n. 4); idem, *Ausgewählte Abhandlungen zur europäischen Reformations- und Konfessionsgeschichte*, ed. Luise Schorn-Schütte and Olaf Mörke (Berlin: Duncker & Humblot, 2002); idem, *Religion, Political Culture, and the Emergence of Early Modern Society: Essays in German and Dutch History* (Leiden: E. J. Brill, 1992); idem, *Civic Calvinism in Northwestern Germany and the Netherlands, Sixteenth to Nineteenth Centuries* (Kirksville, Mo.: Sixteenth Century Journal Publishers, 1991); idem, "Confessional Europe," in *Handbook of European History, 1400–1600: Late Middle Ages, Renaissance and Reformation*, ed. Thomas A. Brady, Heiko A. Oberman, and James D. Tracy (Leiden: E. J. Brill, 1995), 2:641–681.

3. See note 3 to chapter 1 above. For critical remarks and evaluation by a theologian, see Thomas Kaufmann, "Die Konfessionalisierung von Kirche und Gesellschaft. Sammelbericht über eine

Forschungsdebatte," *Theologische Literaturzeitung* 121 (1996): 1,009–1,025 and 1,112–1,121. For a short but dense and extensively annotated discussion in English, see Susan R. Boettcher, "Confessionalization, Reformation, Religion, Absolutism, and Modernity," *History Compass* 2 (2004): 1–10; Joachim Bahlcke and Arno Strohmeyer, eds., *Konfessionalisierung in Ostmitteleuropa: Wirkungen des religiösen Wandels im 16. und 17. Jahrhundert in Staat, Gesellschaft und Kultur* (Stuttgart: Franz Steiner, 1999); Kaspar von Greyerz et al., eds., *Interkonfessionalität – Transkonfessionalität – Binnenkonfessionelle Pluralität: Neue Forschungen zur Konfessionalisierungsthese* (Gütersloh: GTVH, 2003). For a concise historiographical essay, see Stefan Ehrenpreis and Ute Lotz-Heumann, *Reformation und konfessionelles Zeitalter* (Darmstadt: Wissenschaftliche Buchgesellschaft, 2002).

4. Denis Crouzet, *Les guerriers de dieu: La violence au temps des troubles de religion (vers 1525–vers 1610)*, 2 vols. (Seyssel, France: Champ Vallon, 1990).

5. See chapter 4.

6. This concept was held mainly by early modern German lawyers and theologians: for example, Petrus à Beeck in his history of the imperial town of Aix-La Chapelle: "Civitatem dictam aiunt, quasi civium unitatem . . . eodem velle, eodem nolle, eiusdem fidei symbolo . . . coalescere cives"; Petrus à Beeck, *Aquisgranum* (Aix-la Chapelle, 1620), 1. It means that there can only be a civic society if all members adhere to the same symbols of their belief. For a general description of the confessional situation in Germany, see Klaus Schreiner, "Iuramentum religionis. Entstehung, Geschichte und Funktion des Konfessionseides der Staats- und Kirchendiener im Territorialstaat der frühen Neuzeit," *Der Staat* 24 (1985): 211–346; and with regard to one of the leading Lutheran political thinkers, see Horst Dreizel, *Protestantischer Aristotelismus und absoluter Staat: Die "Politica" des Henning Arnisaeus (1575–1636)* (Wiesbaden: Franz Steiner, 1970), esp. 380–392. The maxim "religio vinculum societatis" was common in Europe during the confessional era, and expressed, for example, in England by Bishop Edwin Sandys in the middle of the sixteenth century. To him there was no doubt that "this liberty, that men may openly profess the diversity of religion, must needs be dangerous to the

Commonwealth. . . . One God, one king, one faith, one profession, is fit for one monarchy and commonwealth. . . . Let conformity and unity in religion be provided for; and it shall be as a wall of defence unto this realm"; quoted in *Religion and Society in Early Modern Europe, 1500–1800*, ed. Kaspar von Greyerz (London: Allen and Unwin, 1984), 146. Even the *Commonwealth* of Thomas Hobbes is based on uniformity: not the confessional, dogmatic uniformity of the individual belief of its subjects, but uniformity in public worship, ordained by the sovereign; Thomas Hobbes, "Leviathan. Or the Matter, Form, and Power of a Commonwealth Ecclesiastical and Civil," in his *Collected Works*, ed. Sir William Molesworth (London: Routledge Thoemmes Press, 1994), 3:311, 349, 355–356. See also Ulrich Scheuner, "Staatsräson und religiöse Einheit des Staates," in *Staatsräson: Studien zur Bedeutungsgeschichte eines Wortes*, ed. Roman Schnur (Berlin: Duncker & Humblot, 1973), 363–406. For extensive methodological and theoretical reflections on the role and function of religion and confession in early modern society, see the introduction to my *Konfessionskonflikt und Staatsbildung: Eine Fallstudie über das Verhältnis von religiösem und sozialem Wandel in der Frühneuzeit am Beispiel der Grafschaft Lippe* (Gütersloh: Gütersloher Verlagshaus, 1981), 15–39.

7. The cultural impact of confessionalization has been discussed extensively with regard to the Lutheran confession by the Göttingen church historian Thomas Kaufmann: Thomas Kaufmann, *Konfession und Kultur* (Tübingen: Mohr/Siebeck, 2006); idem, *Dreißigjähriger Krieg und Westfälischer Friede: Kirchengeschichtliche Studien zur lutherischen Konfessionskultur* (Tübingen: Mohr/Siebeck 1998).

8. The following is discussed in more detail and with extensive annotation in Heinz Schilling, "Confessione e identità politica in Europa agli inizi dell'età moderna (XV–XVIII secolo)," *Concilium — rivista internazionale di teologia* 6 (1995): 970–983; idem, "Nationale Identität und Konfession in der europäischen Neuzeit," in *Nationale und kulturelle Identität: Studien zur Entwicklung des kollektiven Bewußtseins in der Neuzeit* ed. Bernhard Giesen (Frankfurt am Main: Suhrkamp, 1991), 192–252. From the perspective of sociology, see Bernd Giesen and Philip Gorski, eds., *Religion and Nation*, conference proceedings, University of Konstanz, July

2006 (forthcoming 2008), with contributions by Shmuel N. Eisenstadt, Thomas Luckmann, Heinz Schilling, Zeev Sternhell, Björn Wittrock, and others.

9. There is extensive literature on this field of research. See Herman Roodenburg and Pieter Spierenburg, eds., *Social Control in Europe, 1500–1800* (Columbus: Ohio State University Press, 2004); Heinz Schilling, ed., *Institutions, Instruments and Agents of Social Control and Discipline in Early Modern Europe* (Frankfurt am Main: Vittorio Klostermann, 1999); Paolo Prodi, ed., *Disciplina dell'anima, disciplina del corpo e disciplina della società tra medioevo et età moderna* (Bologna: Mulino, 1994). With regard to the specific contribution of the confessional churches, see Bruce Gordon, *Clerical Discipline and the Rural Reformation: The Synod in Zürich, 1532–1580* (Bern: Peter Lang, 1992); Raymond A. Mentzer, ed., *Sin and the Calvinists: Morals, Control and the Consistory in the Reformed Tradition* (Kirksville, Mo.: Sixteenth Century Journal Publishers, 1994); Heinz Schilling, ed., *Kirchenzucht und Sozialdisziplinierung im frühneuzeitlichen Europa* (with a selected bibliography) (Berlin: Duncker & Humblot, 1994). For theoretical and methodological considerations, see Heinz Schilling, " 'History of Crime' or 'History of Sin'?—Some Reflections on the Social History of Early Modern Church Discipline," in *Politics and Society in Reformation Europe: Essays for Sir Geoffrey Elton on his 65th Birthday*, ed. E. J. Kouri and T. Scott (London: Macmillan, 1987), 289–310.

10. Louis Châtellier, *L'Europe des dévots* (Paris: Flammarion, 1987), 127, 151; idem, *Le catholicisme en France: le 16e et 17e siècles*, 2 vols. (Paris: SEDES, 1995); idem, *The Religion of the Poor: Rural Missions in Europe and the Formation of Modern Catholicism, 1500–1800* (Cambridge: Cambridge University Press, 1997); Heinz Schilling, "Calvinist and Catholic Cities—Urban Architecture and Rituals in Confessional Europe," *European Review* 3 (2004): 293–312. For general commentary on the social and cultural impact of confessionalization, see Wolfgang Reinhard and Heinz Schilling, eds., *Die Katholische Konfessionalisierung* (Gütersloh: Gütersloher Verlagshaus, 1995).

11. Eszter Andor and István György Tóth, eds., *Frontiers of Faith: Religious Exchange and the Constitution of Religious Identi-*

ties 1400–1750 (Budapest: Central European University / European Science Foundation, 2001); Maria Craciun and Ovidio Ghitta, ed., *Church and Society in Central and Eastern Europe* (Cluj-Napoka, Romania: European Studies Foundation, 1998); Heinz Schilling and István György Tóth, eds., *Religious and Cultural Exchange in Europe, 1400–1750* (Cambridge: Cambridge University Press, 2007).

12. Hans-Jürgen Görtz and James M. Stayer, *Radikalität und Dissent im 16. Jahrhundert / Radicalism and Dissent in the Sixteenth Century* (Berlin: Duncker & Humblot, 2002); see also the proceedings of a summer 2006 conference at Göttingen, in Anselm Schubert's *Grenzen des Täufertums: Forschungsperspektiven in der Internationalen Täuferforschung* (Gütersloh, forthcoming).

13. For the first considerations on that topic, see Gerhard Lauer, "Die Konfessionalisierung des Judentums. Zum Prozeß der religiösen Ausdifferenzierung im Judentum am Übergang zur Neuzeit," in von Greyerz et al., eds., *Interkonfessionalität* (note 3).

14. Leszek Kołakowski, *Chrétiens sans église: La conscience religieuse et le lien confessionel au 17e siècle* (Paris: Gallimard, 1969).

15. For Poland, see Janusz Taszbir, *A State without Stakes. Polish Religious Toleration in the 16th and 17th Centuries* (Warsaw: Panstwowy Instytut Wydawniczy, 1973), though there is evidently need for a "modernization" of the Polish religious history of the sixteenth century along the historiographical lines sketched in the text of my lectures. Out of a vast literature on the Netherlands, the following are especially helpful: Willem Frijhoff, *Embodied Belief: Ten Essays of Religious Culture in Dutch History* (Hilversum, the Netherlands: Verloren, 2002); Judith Pollmann, *Religious Choice in the Dutch Republic: The Reformation of Arnoldus Buchelius (1565–1641)* (Manchester: Manchester University Press, 1999); Wiebe Bergsma, "Church, State, and People," in *A Miracle Mirrored: The Dutch Republic in European Perspective*, ed. Karel Davids and Jan Lucassen (Cambridge: Cambridge University Press, 1995), 196–228.

16. Johannes Kühn, *Toleranz und Offenbarung* (Leipzig: Meiner, 1923).

17. Marc Greengrass, Michael Leslie, and Timothy Raylor, eds.,

Samuel Hartlib and Universal Reformation: Studies in Intellectual Communication (Cambridge: Cambridge University Press, 1994); most innovative and characterized by deep erudition are the works in this field by Howard Hotson, *Johann Heinrich Alsted, 1588–1638: Between Renaissance, Reformation, and Universal Reform* (Oxford: Oxford University Press, 2000); idem, "Irenicism in the Confessional Age: The Holy Roman Empire, 1563–1648," in *Conciliation and Confession: Struggling for Unity in the Age of Reform, 1415–1648,* ed. Howard Louthan and Randall Zachman (Notre Dame, Ind.: University of Notre Dame Press, 2004), 228–285; idem, "Irenicism and Dogmatics in the Confessional Age: Pareus and Comenius in Heidelberg 1614," *Journal of Ecclesiastical History* 46 (1995): 432–456; with particular regard to the attitude toward Jews, see idem, "Antisemitismus, Philosemitismus und Chiliasmus im frühneuzeitlichen Europa," *Werkstatt Geschichte* 24 (1999): 7–35.

18. The exchange and transfer of ideas first became substantial in the Netherlands around the second third of the seventeenth century, and at the end of the century in England, whereas owing in large part to the petrification of confessionalism after the Peace of Westphalia, the situation of the Jewish community in Germany remained more or less isolated, though on a fairly well ordered legal basis. Basic with regard to the Netherlands are the publications of Yosef Kaplan, *From Christianity to Judaism: The Story of Isaac Orobio de Castro,* translated from the Hebrew by Raphael Loese (New York: published for the Littman Library by Oxford University Press, 1989); idem, *An Alternative Path to Modernity: The Sephardi Diaspora in Western Europe* (Leiden: Brill, 2000). For a comprehensive view with regard to Germany, see Friedrich Battenberg, *Die Juden in Deutschland vom 16. bis zum Ende des 18. Jahrhunderts* (München: Oldenbourg, 2001); concerning their legal status, see idem, "Des Kaisers Kammerknechte. Gedanken zur rechtlich-sozialen Situation der Juden in Spätmittelalter und Früher Neuzeit," *Historische Zeitschrift* 245 (1987): 545–599; idem, "Die Privilegierung von Juden und der Judenschaft im Bereich des Heiligen Römischen Reiches," in *Das Privileg im europäischen Vergleich,* ed. Barbara Dölemeyer and Horst Mohnhaupt, (Frankfurt am Main: Klostermann, 1996), 1:139–190. A good case study for the situation

in the Imperial city of Frankfort is Stephan Wendehorst's "Die Kaiserhuldigungen der Frankfurter Juden im 18. Jahrhundert," in *Die Frankfurter Judengasse. Jüdisches Leben in der Frühen Neuzeit*, ed. Fritz Backhaus et al. (Frankfurt am Main: Societätsverlag, 2006), 213–235, 239–245. Notably this legal security within the multiconfessional Reich gave some Jewish observers the impression of a tolerant situation in Germany, as is documented by an 1818 statement of the enlightened German Jew Saul Ascher: "Deutschland stellt gewiß das erste Beispiel von Duldung auf; denn die Nation selbst gestand es sich zu, in religiöser Hinsicht verschiedener Meinung sein zu dürfen. . . . Es ist ganz natürlich der Erfolg gewesen, daß die Duldung, die sich die Nation in Glaubenssachen zugestand, auch herabwirkte auf diejenigen, die überhaupt nicht christlichen Glaubens waren und daß daher in Deutschland stillschweigend der Geist der Toleranz bis ins 18. Jahrhundert eine vorzüglichere Ausbildung erhielt," Saul Ascher, *Die Wartburgs-Feier. Mit Hinsicht auf Deutschlands religiöse und politische Stimmung* (Leipzig: Aschenwall, 1818), 41–42, as quoted in Stephan Wendehorst, "Advocati Imperatoris Judaica—Der Kaiser, das Reich und die Juden in der Frühen Neuzeit," in *Lesebuch Altes Reich*, ed. Stephan Wendehorst and Siegrid Westphal (München: Oldenbourg, 2006), 222–229.

19. Quote from Diethelm Klippel, "Souveränität," in *Geschichtliche Grundbegriffe: Historisches Lexikon zur politisch-sozialen Sprache in Deutschland* (Stuttgart: Klett-Cotta, 1990), 6:108, n. 65. See in the same work, "Toleranz," by Klaus Schreiner, 6:545–594.

20. Notably this development started in the Netherlands with its multiconfessional culture and an active osmosis between Christianity and Judaism. Next to Spinoza's work the publications of Jan and Pieter de la Court are crucial: *Het welvaeren van Leiden, 1659*, ed. Felix Driessen (The Hague: Martinus Nejhoff, 1911; French trans. by Madeleine Francis, *La Balance politique* [Paris: Félix Alcan, 1936]). For the context of political thinking at that period, see Heinz Schilling, "Der libertär-radikale Republikanismus der holländischen Regenten. Ein Beitrag zur Geschichte des politischen Radikalismus in der frühen Neuzeit," *Geschichte und Gesellschaft* 10 (1984): 498–533, esp. 528–533.

21. Pictures in Hans Galen, ed., *Der Westfälische Frieden — Die*

Friedensmedaillen, (Münster: Stadtmuseum, 1988), 179, no. 160; 197, no. 182, 182A; 153, no. 129.

III. Migration and Minorities

1. Carlo N. Cipolla, "The Diffusion of Innovations in Early Modern Europe," *Comparative Studies in Society and History* 14 (1972): 46–52; idem, *For the Industrial Revolution: European Society and Economy, 1000–1700* (London: Methuen, 1976), 174–181.

2. For a comprehensive overview, see Nicholas P. Canny, ed., *Europeans on the Move: Studies in European Migration, 1500–1800* (Oxford: Oxford University Press, 1994); Etienne François, ed., *Immigrations et société urbaine en Europe oxidentale XVIe–XXe siècles* (Paris: Editions Rechereche sur les Civilisations, 1985); Simonetta Cavaciocchi, ed., *Le migrazioni in Europa, Secc. XIII–XVIII* (Florence: Le Monnier, 1994); Leslie Page Moch, *Moving Europeans: Migration in Western Europe since 1650* (Bloomington: Indiana University Press, 2003); Klaus J. Bade, *Europa in Bewegung: Migration vom späten 18. Jahrhunderts bis zur Gegenwart* (München: Beck, 2000; English and French translations available).

3. Heinz Schilling, "Die frühneuzeitliche Konfessionsmigration," in *Migration in der europäischen Geschichte seit dem späten Mittelalter*, ed. Klaus J. Bade (Osnabrück: Universitätsverlag Rasch, 2002), 67–89.

4. See figure 40 in Jean-Pierre Bardet and Jacques Dupâquier, eds., *Histoire des populations de l'Europe* (Paris: Fayard, 1997).

5. Gabriel Audisio, *Les "Vaudios": Naissance, vie et mort d'une dissidence, 12e–16e siècles* (Turin: Albert Meynier, 1989); idem, *Une grande migration Alpine in Provence (1460–1560)* (Turin: Deputazione Subalpina di storia patria, 1989); idem, *Die Waldenser. Die Geschichte einer religiösen Bewegung* (München: Beck, 1996).

6. There is no general comprehensive work on this movement, but dozens of monographs and articles on specific branches, regions, or cities exist, only a few of which can be listed here. For a typological essay, see Heinz Schilling, "Confessional Migration as a Distinct Type of Old European Longdistance Migration," in *Le migrazioni*, ed. Cavaciocchi (above, note 2), 175–189; idem and

Marie-Antoinette Gross, eds., *Im Spannungsfeld von Staat und Kir-che: "Minderheiten" und "Erziehung" im deutsch-französischen Gesellschaftsvergleich, 16.–18. Jahrhundert* (Berlin: Duncker & Humblot, 2003). With regard to the Netherlands, see the review article by Gustaaf Janssens, "Verjaagd uit Nederland: Zuidneder-landse Emigratie in de zestiende eeuw," *Nederlands archif voor Kerkgeschiedenis* (1995): 102–119; Willem Frijhoff, "Migrations re-ligieuses dans les Provinces-Unies avant le Second Refuge," *Revue du Nord* 80 (1998): 573–598; for a general overview, see Jan Lucas-sen and Rinus Penninx, *Newcomers: Immigrants and Their Dissi-dences in the Netherlands, 1550–1995* (Amsterdam: Het Sbinhuis, 1997). With regard to Germany, see Klaus J. Bade, ed., *Deutsche im Ausland, Fremde in Deutschland: Migration in Geschichte und Gegenwart* (München: Beck, 1992), esp. the contribution of Heinz Duchhardt, 278–286; Alexander Schunka, "Glaubensflucht als Mig-rationsoption. Konfessionell motivierte Migrationen in der frühen Neuzeit," *Geschichte in Wissenschaft und Unterricht* 56 (2005): 547–564; Werner Wilhelm Schnabel, *Österreichische Exulanten in oberdeutschen Reichsstädten* (München: Beck, 1992); Rudolf Leeb, Susanne C. Pils, and Thomas Winkelbauer, eds., *Staatsmacht und Seelenheil. Gegenreformation und Geheimprotestantismus in der Habsburgermonarchie* (Wien: Oldenbourg, 2007): chapters 5 and 6 on persecution and exile, 181–270. For a comprehensive treatment of the Hugenots, see Myriam Yardeni, *Le refuge protestante* (Paris: PUF, 1985). On Italian refugees, see Simonetta Adorni Braccesi and Carla Sodini, eds., *L'emigrazione confessionale dei lucchesi in Eu-ropa* (Florence: Edifir, 1999); on the Salzburgians, see Mac Walker, *Der Salzburger Handel: Vertreibung und Errettung der Salzburger Protestanten im 18. Jahrhundert* (Göttingen: Vandenhoeck, 1997).

7. For a general overview, see Jonathan Irvine Israel, *European Jewry in the Age of Mercantilism, 1550–1750* (London and Port-land, Ore.: Littman Library of Jewish Civilization, 1998), esp. chap-ter 1 "Exodus from the West," 1–28. See also Henry Méchoulan, ed., *Les judíos de España. Historia de una diaspora, 1492–1992* (Madrid: Trotta, 1993); Elisheva Carlebach, "European Jewry in the Early Modern Period: 1492–1750," in *The Oxford Handbook of Jewish Studies*, ed. Martin Goodman (Oxford: Oxford Univer-sity Press, 2002), 363–375; Yosef Kaplan, *An Alternative Path to*

Modernity: The Sephardi Diaspora in Western Europe, vol. 28 of Brill's Series in Jewish Studies (Leiden: Brill, 2000); Sarah Abrevaya Stein, "Sephardi and Middle Eastern Jewries since 1492," in *The Oxford Handbook of Jewish Studies*, ed. Martin Goodman (Oxford: Oxford University Press, 2002), 327–362.

8. For example, there is no specific article on this phenomenon in Bardet and Dupâquier, *Histoire des populations* (note 4).

9. See P. Clark and P. Slack, *English Towns in Transition, 1500–1700* (Oxford: Oxford University Press, 1976); P. Clark, "Migration in England during the late 17th and early 18th centuries," *Past and Present*, 83 (1979): 57–90. Jan de Vries, *European Urbanization, 1500–1800* (London: Methuen, 1984), who refers strongly to migration, is not at all concerned with the religiously motivated demographic movements of the sixteenth to the eighteenth centuries; the same is true of Paul M. Hohenberg and Lyn Hollen Lies, *The Making of Urban Europe, 1000–1950* (Cambridge, Mass.: Harvard University Press, 1985), who only touched upon the religious dimension briefly (p. 94); only Etienne François, closely familiar with the situation in multiconfessional early modern Germany, pays more attention to the religious factor within the Old European migration scene: François, "Immigration et société urbaine en Allemagne à l'époque moderne (17e–18e siècle). Remarques sur deux types de politique de l'immigration," in *Habiter la ville (XVe–XXe siècles*, ed. M. Garden and Y. Lequin (Lyon: Presse universitaires de Lyon, 1985).

10. Heinz Schilling, "Confessional Migration" (note 6).

11. For the Peace of Augsburg in general and the question of religious minorities and migrants, see Heinz Schilling and Heribert Smolinsky, eds., *Der Augsburger Religionsfrieden 1555* (Gütersloh: Gütersloher Verlagshaus, 2007), especially the contribution of Mathias Asche.

12. Helmuth Kreßner, *Schweizer Ursprünge des anglikanischen Staatskirchentums* (Gütersloh: Gütersloher Verlagshaus, 1953).

13. Figures from Audisio, *Waldenser* (see above, note 5), 81–85; Heinz Schilling, *Niederländische Exulanten im 16. Jahrhundert. Ihre Stellung im Sozialgefüge und im religiösen Leben deutscher und englischer Städte* (Gütersloh: Gütersloher Verlagshaus, 1972); and Frijhoff, *Migrations* (note 6), 587f.; Fernand Donnet, "Les exiles

anversoirs à Cologne (1582–1585)," *Bulletin de l'Académie royale d'archéologie de Belgique* 5. sér. 1 (1898): 288–355; Schnabel, *Österreichische Exulanten* (note 6), 71, 647; Yardeni, *Refuge* (note 6), 49; Duchhardt, in *Deutsche im Ausland*, ed. Bade (note 6), 282; Adorni-Braccesi and Sodini, *L'emigrazione* (note 6), 22; Méchoulan, *Judios* (note 7) and Hiltrud Wallenborn, *Bekehrungseifer, Judenangst und Handelsinteresse: Amsterdam, Hamburg und London als Ziele sefardischer Migration im 17. Jahrhundert* (Hildesheim: Georg Olms, 2003), 11–17.

14. Figures from Schilling, *Niederländische Exulanten* (note 13), 179; Frijhoff, *Migrations* (note 6), 590; Sibylle Badstübner-Gröger, ed., *Hugenotten in Berlin* (Berlin: Union Verlag, 1988), 66.

15. There is no article on Huguenots in *Les Lieux de mémoire*, ed. Pierre Nora, but under the headline "minorités religieuses" there is an article by Philippe Joutard "Le musée du Désert" (2:530–560); even in the German version, *Erinnerungsorte*, ed. Etienne François and Hagen Schulze, 3 vols. (München: Beck, 1985) there is no article on Huguenots, even though these refugees are part of Germany's identity, esp. in Brandenburg-Prussia. In Berlin, the Huguenots are represented prominently in lectures, conferences, and exhibitions. The most recent exhibition was at the German Historical Museum in 2005; see the exhibition catalogue *Zuwanderungsland Deutschland. Die Hugenotten*, ed. Sabine Bennecke and Hans Ottomeyer (Wolfratshausen: Minerva, 2005).

16. The Catholic branch, admittedly very small, of the emigration from the Burgenland provinces is only poorly researched. See Donnet, *Les exiles* (note 13); see also Joachim Deeters and Klaus Militzer, eds., *Belgien in Köln*, exhibition catalogue (Köln: Historisches Archiv, 1981), 71–106.

17. Andrew Pettegree, who tends to offer low figures, estimates only thirty to sixty thousand for the 1566/1567 wave; see Andrew Pettegree, *Emden and the Dutch Revolt: Exile and the Development of Reformed Protestantism* (Oxford: Clarendon, 1992), 148. My own statistics are in my *Niederländische Exulanten* (note 13), 175–180 with a bibliography of the older literature. For a case study on London, see Andrew Pettegree, *Foreign Protestant Communities in Sixteenth-Century London* (Oxford: Oxford University Press, 1986); for a general treatment of England, see Raingard

Eßer, *Niederländische Exulanten im England des 16. und frühen 17. Jahrhunderts* (Berlin: Ducker & Humblot, 1996).

18. For a basic treatment, see Kaplan, *Alternative Path* (note 7); idem, *From Christianity* (above, chap. 2, note 18); Wallenborn, *Bekehrungseifer* (note 13); for a general overview, see Jonathan I. Israel, *European Jewry in the Age of Mercantilism, 1550–1750*, 3rd ed. (London and Portland, Ore.: Littman Library of Jewish Civilization, 1998), 4–57. For an essay on longterm development, see Rob van Engeldorp Gastelaars et al., "Jewish Amsterdam 1600–1940: from 'Ghetto' to 'neighbourhoods,'" in François, *Immigration* (note 2), 127–141.

19. Kaplan, *Alternative Path* (note 7), 81.

20. On the numbers of Jews from the Iberian peninsula see Wallenborn, *Bekehrungseifer* (note 13), 17; on the numbers for the Christian minorities from the Netherlands see Schilling, *Niederländische Exulanten* (note 14), 179.

21. Wilfried Brulyez, *De Firma Della Faille en de internationale handel van vlaamse firma's in de 16ᵉ eeuw* (Brussels: n.p., 1959); idem, "De diaspora der antwerpse kooplui op het einde van de 16ᵉ eeuw," *Bejdragen voor de geschiedenis der Nederlanden* 15 (1960): 279–306.

22. Wallenborn, *Bekehrungseifer* (note 13), 15.

23. For the situation of the Christian minorities in Frankfurt and Hamburg, see Schilling, *Exulanten* (note 14), 52–59, 121–124, 131–133; for the Sephardim community at Hamburg, see Wallenborn, *Bekehrungseifer* (note 13), 21 ff.; Wallenborn does not reflect on the simultaneous conflicts between Lutheran citizens and Calvinist migrants. On the general social and political situation in German cities in early modern times, see Heinz Schilling, *Die Stadt in der frühen Neuzeit*, 2nd ed. (München: Oldenbourg, 2004). The stranger communities in Frankfurt in particular are excellently documented in several sources: Hermann Meinert and Wolfram Dahmer, eds., *Das Protokollbuch der niederländischen reformierten Gemeinde zu Frankfurt am Main, 1570–1581* (Frankfurt am Main: Waldemar Kramer, 1977); Hermann Meinert, *Die Eingliederung der niederländischen Glaubensflüchtlinge in die Frankfurter Bürgerschaft, 1554–1596* (Frankfurt am Main: Waldemar Kramer, 1981); Abraham Mangon, *Kurze, doch wahrhaftige Beschreibung*

der Geschichte der Reformierten in Frankfurt, 1554–1712, ed. Irene Dingel (Leipzig: Evang. Verlagsanstalt, 2004).

24. This micromigration within the greater Hamburg area is well expressed in the title of an early monograph on the Jewish minority of this region: Hermann Kellenbenz's 1958 book is not titled Sephardim in Hamburg but Sephardim an der unteren Elbe: Ihre wirtschaftliche und politische Bedeutung vom Ende des 16. bis zum Beginn des 18. Jahrhunderts (Wiesbaden: Steiner, 1958).

25. For a general perspective of the crises in the "Reich" around 1600, see Heinz Schilling, Aufbruch und Krise: Deutschland, 1517–1648, 2nd ed. (Berlin: Siedler, 1994), 382–385.

26. This context is well researched with regard to the idea of a poor, godly community in Puritan England. With regard to Continental Calvinism, see my article in Schilling and Tóth, Religion and Cultural Exchange (chapter 2, note 11) on purity of the Lord's Supper celebration or on impurity in consequence of homosexuality or sodomy (which were regarded as "sin against nature and salvation").

27. See chapter 2, note 6.

28. Overview in Schilling, Aufbruch (note 25), 371–419.

29. This is the argument by the Frankfort magistrate (1608) against the construction of a Calvinist church building on city grounds; quoted by F. Scharff, "Die Niederlande und französische Gemeinde Frankfurt am Main," Archiv für Frankfurts Geschichte und Kunst, n.s. 2 (1862): 245–318, here 292.

30. For a basic treatment of the pogrom and the new legal order, see Isidor Kracauer, Geschichte der Juden in Frankfurt am Main, 1150–1824, 2 vols (Frankfurt am Main: In Kommission bei I. Kauffmann, 1925–1927); for a wide perspective on urban constitution and burgher protest, see Mathias Meyn, Die Reichsstadt Frankfurt vor dem Bürgeraufstand von 1612–1614: Struktur und Krise (Frankfurt am Main: Waldemar Kramer, 1990), on the Jews in particular, 51 ff.; Gerald Lyman Soliday, A Community in Conflict: Frankfurt Society in the 17th and Early 18th Centuries (Hanover, N.H: University Press of New England, 1974), 175–197 on the legal basis and social situation of Jewish community; Christopher Friedrichs, "German Town Revolts and the Seventeenth-Century Crisis," Renaissance and Modern Studies 26 (1982): 51–71; idem., "Urban Conflicts

and the Imperial Constitution in Seventeenth-Century Germany," *Journal of Modern History* 58 (1986): 98–123; Robert Brandt et al., *Der Fettmilch-Aufstand: Bürgerunruhen und Judenfeindschaft in Frankfurt am Main, 1612–1616* (Frankfurt am Main: Verlag, 1996); a recent penetrating interpretation is Wendehorst's, *Kaiserhuldigungen* (chapter 2, note 18), esp. 228 ff. On the general situation in German cities around 1600, see Schilling, *Stadt* (note 23).

31. For the origin of the Sephardi congregation at London after the collapse of the Dutch colonies at Brazil, see Jonathan I. Israel, "Menasseh ben Israel and the Dutch Sephardi Colonisation Movement of the Mid-Seventeenth Century (1645–1657)," in Yoseph Kaplan et al., eds., *Menasseh ben Israel and his World* (Leiden: Brill, 1989), 130–163; Yoseph Kaplan, "The Jewish Profile of the Spanish-Portuguese Community in London during the Seventeenth Century," in idem, *Alternative Path* (note 7), 155–167; Wallenborn, *Bekehrungseifer* (note 15).

32. Analyzed in detail by Schilling, *Exulanten* (note 14), 152–174; the segregation of the Jewish community at Amsterdam is stressed by Engeldorp Gastelaars, "Jewish Amsterdam" (note 18), 129–131.

33. Johann Wolfgang von Goethe, *Aus meinem Leben. Dichtung und Wahrheit*, part 4, end of 17th book.

34. Kaplan, *Alternative Path* (note 7), passim, 50 ff.

35. On the theological roots, see Glenn S. Sunshine, "Reformed Theology and the Origins of Synodical Polity: Calvin, Beza and the Gallican Confession," in *Later Calvinism: International Perspectives*, ed. W. Fred Graham (Kirksville, Mo.: Sixteenth Century Journal Publishers, 1994), 141–158; essential treatments of the organization of church government in Geneva are the articles and books of Robert M. Kingdon, esp. his edition of the *Registres du Consistoire de Genève au temps de Calvin*, 3 vols. (Geneva: DROZ, 1996–2004), preface and introduction vii–xxviii; for a treatment of the church organization in Emden, and the influence of the church organization in Northwestern Europe in general, see Heinz Schilling, ed., *Die Kirchenratsprotokolle der reformierten Gemeinde Emden, 1557–1620*, 2 vols. (Köln and Wien: Böhlau, 1989 and 1992), introduction, viii–xxviii.

36. See the editions organized by Robert M. Kingdon and Heinz

Schilling, above, note 35. The prosopography and the governing activities of the refugee churches are analyzed in Heinz Schilling, *Civic Calvinism in Northwestern Germany and the Netherlands, Sixteenth to Nineteenth Centuries* (Kirksville, Mo.: Sixteenth Century Journal Publishers, 1991); idem, *Ausgewählte Abhandlungen zur europäischen Reformations- und Konfessionsgeschichte*, ed. Luise Schorn-Schütte and Olaf Mörke (Berlin: Duncker & Humblot, 2002); idem, "Reform and Supervision of Family Life in Germany and the Netherlands," in *Sin and the Calvinists: Morals Control and the Consistory in the Reformed Tradition*, ed. Raymond A. Mentzer (Kirksville, Mo.: Sixteenth Century Journal Publishers, 1994), 15–61. For general literature on social discipline and social control, see above, chapter 2, note 9.

37. The following considerations of the Jewish communities are based mainly on the work of Yosef Kaplan, *From Christianity* and *Alternative Path* (chapter 2, note 17).

38. On the protocols on the Emden Presbytery, see Heinz Schilling, "Reformierte Kirchenzucht als Sozialdisziplinierung? Die Tätigkeit des Emder Presbyteriums in den Jahren 1557–1562," in: *Niederlande und Nordwestdeutschland*, ed. Wilfried Ehbrecht and Heinz Schilling (Köln and Wien: Böhlau, 1983).

39. Schilling, *Kirchenratsprotokolle* (note 34), 1:148 n. 13.

40. In this respect parallels to the sexual discipline of the Sephardic congregation at Amsterdam as described by Kaplan seem especially obvious; see Yosef Kaplan, "The Threat of Eros in Eighteenth-Century Sephardi Amsterdam," in idem, *Alternative Path* (note 7), 280–300.

41. Ibid., 26.

42. See "The Discussion of Techniques" in Carlo M. Chipolla's *Before the Industrial Revolution* (London: Methuen, 1976), 174–181; see also above, note 1).

43. As in the present context we can neither give a general overview nor details of the economic impact for the respective European societies. The reader interested in this particular field might consult the following literature, most of it containing further bibliographical information: Frederick Norwood, *The Reformation Refugees as an Economic Force* (Chicago: American Society of Church History, 1942); J. G. C. A. Briels, *Zuid-Nederlanders*

in de Republiek, 1572–1630 (Sint-Niklaas, 1985); idem, "De Zuid-Nederlandse immigratie omstreeks, 1572–1630," *Tijdschrift voor geschiedenis* 100 (1987): 331–354.

44. Johannes Kernkamp, *Handel op den vijand*, 2 vols. (Utrecht: Keminko, 1931 and 1934).

45. See chapter 2.

46. Hermann Kellenbenz, ed., *Zwei Jahrtausende Kölner Wirtschaft*, vol. 1 (Köln: Greven, 1975), esp. 481–487; Barbara Becker-Jákli, *Die Protestanten in Köln: Entwicklung einer Minderheit* (Köln: Rheinland-Verlag, 1983). On the long-term consequences, see Dietrich Ebeling, *Bürgertum und Pöbel: Wirtschaft und Gesellschaft Kölns im 18. Jahrhundert* (Köln and Wien: Böhlau, 1987); H. V. Asten, "Die religiöse Spaltung in der Reichsstadt Aachen und ihr Einfluß auf die industrielle Entwicklung in der Umgebung," *Zeitschrift des Aachener Geschichtsvereins*, 68 (1956): 77–197.

47. There is ample literature on this phenomenon. See, for example, Friedrich Zunkel, "Die Bedeutung des Protestantismus für die industrielle Entwicklung Stolbergs," *Monatshefte für Evangelische Kirchengeschichte des Rheinlandes* 29 (1980): 133–150; Herbert Kisch, *Die hausindustriellen Textilgewerbe am Niederrhein vor der industriellen Revolution* (Göttingen: Vandenhoeck und Ruprecht, 1981). Both authors touch upon the topic of religious minorities and religion as a social factor several times, but they are not very strong on the theological and ecclesiastical aspect. This approach is especially true with regard to the early Calvinist migration (esp. Kisch, *Textilgewerbe*, 97 ff., 264 ff.), whereas the Mennonites are more thoroughly discussed (ibid., 104 ff.)

48. See Heiko Oberman, "Die Reformation als theologische Revolution," in *Zwingli und Europa*, ed. Peter Blickle et al. (Zurich: Vandenhoeck & Ruprecht, 1985), 11–26, esp. 24 f.

49. See Heinz Schilling, "Bürgerkämpfe in Aachen zu Beginn des 17. Jahrhunderts. Konflikte im Rahmen der alteuropäischen Stadtgesellschaft oder im Umkreis der frühbürgerlichen Revolution?" *Zeitschrift für Historische Forschung* 1(1974): 175–231; from the perspective of the imperial court, see Walter Schmitz, *Verfassung und Bekenntnis. Die Aachener Wirren im Spiegel der kaiserlichen Politik, 1550–1614* (Frankfurt am Main: Lang, 1983).

50. Discussed intensively during the 1970s and 1980s by left-

wing social and economic historians, for example, W. Wallerstein and J. Merrington in the *New Left Review*; John Merrington, "Town and Country in the Transition to Capitalism," *New Left Review* 1 (1993) Sept.-Oct. 1975: 71–92, here 80.

51. For the situation in London, see Pettegree, *Foreign Protestant Communities* (note 17); for a short sketch of a Lasco's perambulations, see Menno Smid, "Reisen und Aufenthaltsorte a Lascos," in *Johannes a Lasco (1499–1560). Polnischer Baron, Humanist und europäischer Reformator*, ed. Christoph Strohm (Tübingen: Mohr/ Siebeck, 2000), 187–198, here 194f.; Henning P. Jürgens, *Johannes a Lasco in Ostfriesland* (Tübingen: Mohr/Siebeck, 2002); for more detail, see Frederick A. Norwood, "The London Dutch Refugees in search of a Home, 1553–54," *American Historical Review* 58 (1952–53): 72–74; Karl Möckeberg, "Johannes a Lasco und seiner Fremdengemeinde Aufnahme in Dänemark und Norddeutschland," *Zeitschrift für kirchliche Wissenschaft und kirchliches Leben* 4 (1883): 588–604; Andrew Pettegree, "The London Exile Community and the Second Sacramentarien Controversy, 1553–1660," *Archiv für Reformationsgeschichte* 78 (1987): 223–252. On the reception in Frankfurt in detail, see *Abraham Mangon*, ed. Irene Dingel (note 20), introduction, 11–28, with bibliographical notes on the older literature.

52. A reproduction and explanation of a Lasco's seal are in Strohm, *A Lasco* (note 51) at the inner side of the cover and the back side of the front page; an epitaph with the symbol of the ship of God as representation of the Calvinist foreign churches was erected at the harbor of Emden and was later on transferred to the entrance of the Große Kirche of the city, where it still can be seen today. Reproduction in *Republiek tussen vorsten*, ed. Frouke Wieringa (Zutphen: De Walburg Pers, 1984), 138.

53. Heiko A. Oberman, "Theologische Revolution" (note 43); idem, *Die Reformation: Von Wittenberg nach Genf* (Göttingen: Vandenhoeck & Ruprecht, 1986), part 3, "Eine Epoche—drei Reformationen," 283–300, esp. 296f.; see also his Heineken Lecture "The Devil and the Devious Historian: Reaching for the Roots of Modernity," in *Heineken Lectures 1996* (Amsterdam: Royal Netherlands Academy of Arts and Sciences, 1997), 33–44. For general reflections, see Hans-Martin Kirn, *Identität im Widerspruch: Das Verhältnis von Christentum und Judentum als kirchengeschichtliches*

Thema, Kamper Oraties 20 (Kampen, the Netherlands: Theologische Universität, 2002).

54. Howard Hotson, "Antisemitismus, Philosemitismus und Chiliasmus im neuzeitlichen Europa," *Werkstatt Geschichte* 24 (1999): 7–35. Also, David Katz, *Philo-Semitism and the Readmission of the Jews to England, 1603–1655* (Oxford: Oxford University Press, 1982). I am grateful to a reader for suggesting the latter source.

55. The migration of the Flaccian minority and its symbolic representation by the exul/peregrinus idea is at present under study in the project "Erzwungenes und selbstgewähltes Exil—Migration und Exil im Luthertum des 16. Jahrhunderts" of Professor Irene Dingel and the Institut für Europäische Geschichte at Mainz.

56. There are famous *peregrini* figures in the German literature of the classical and Romantic period, especially Goethe's "Herman und Dorothea" (1897) or Mörike's Peregrina poems in his novel *Maler Nolte* (1833). Their meaning, however, is quite different from the *peregrinus* mentality of the Calvinist refugees of the sixteenth century. A detailed comparison of the two cultural representations of "strangerness" would be very interesting.

57. This declaration of the Nazi bishops of the Deutsche Christen is quoted with understandable disgust on page 100 of Michael Wieck's *Zeugnis vom Untergang Königsbergs: Ein "Geltungsjude" berichtet* (München: Beck, 2005), a very touching and impressive autobiography of a Königsberg Jew who first was persecuted by the Nazis and after the liberation of Königsberg by the Russian Communists. It is important to realize that although this attitude was characteristic of the Nazi branch of German Lutherans, the Deutsche Christen, the branch of resistant Lutherans, represented by Dietrich Bonhoeffer, Martin Niemüller, and the Bekennende Kirche did not share their Nazi antisemitism.

IV. The European Crisis of the Early Seventeenth Century and the Birth of an International State System

1. As I have just finished two books on the rise of the international system during the confessional period, in the following

I dispense with extensive annotation and refer to Heinz Schilling, *Konfessionalisierung und Staatsinteressen. Internationale Beziehungen 1559–1660*, Handbuch der Geschichte der Internationalen Beziehungen, vol. 2 (Paderborn: Schöningh, 2007), and idem, ed., *Konfessioneller Fundamentalismus. Religion als politischer Faktor im europäischen Mächtesystem um 1600* (München: Oldenbourg, 2007)

2. See the first monograph on the basis of the confessionalization approach: Heinz Schilling, *Konfessionskonflikt und Staatsbildung: Eine Fallstudie über das Verhältnis von religiösem und sozialem Wandel in der Frühneuzeit am Beispiel der Grafschaft Lippe* (Gütersloh: G. Mohn, 1981). This early etatistic bias of the confessional paradigm has meanwhile been broadened during the discussions to a broader multiperspective approach with strong emphasis on the cultural consequences of confessionalization. See above, chapter 2.

3. Early modern state building has been recently described in detail by Wolfgang Reinhard in his masterpeace *Die Macht des Staates: Eine vergleichende Verfassungsgeschichte Europas von den Anfängen bis zur Gegenwart* (München: Beck, 1999).

4. Some preliminary considerations on this topic are given in several of my essays, for example, Heinz Schilling, "Konfessionalisierung und Formierung eines internationalen Systems während der frühen Neuzeit," in *Die Reformation in Deutschland und Europa: Interpretationen und Debatten*, ed. H. Guggisberg and G. Krodel (Gütersloh: Güterslsoher Verlagshaus, 1993), 597–613; idem, "Die konfessionellen Glaubenskriege und die Formierung des frühmodernen Europa," in *Glaubenskriege in Vergangenheit und Gegenwart*, ed. Peter Herrmann (Göttingen: Vandenhoeck & Ruprecht, 1996), 123–137; idem, "War and Peace at the Emergence of Modernity: Europe between State Belligerence, Religious War and the Desire for Peace," in *1648 — War and Peace in Europe: Politics, Religion, Law and Society*, ed. Klaus Bußmann and Heinz Schilling (Münster: Veranstaltungsges. 350 Jahre Westfälischer Frieden, 1998), 13–22; idem, "La confessionalisation et le système international," in *L'Europe des traités de Westphalie. Esprit de la diplomatie et diplomatie de l'esprit*, ed. Lucien Bély (Paris: Presses Universitaires de France, 2000), 411–428.

5. Heinz Schilling, "Gab es um 1600 in Europa einen Konfessionsfundamentalismus? Die Geburt des internationalen Systems in der Krise des konfessionellen Zeitalters," in *Jahrbuch des Historischen Kollegs 2005* (München: Oldenbourg, 2006), 69–93.

6. Described in detail in Heinz Schilling, "Formung und Gestalt des Internationalen Systems in der werdenden Neuzeit—Phasen und bewegende Kräfte," in *Kontinuität und Wandel in der Staatenordnung der Neuzeit. Beiträge zur Geschichte des internationalen Systems*, ed. Peter Krüger (Marburg: Hitzeroth, 1991),19–45.

7. This struggle for a new concept of political order between the rising European states is part of the much wider "struggle for stability," described so brilliantly by Theodore Karl Rabb in his *The Struggle for Stability in Early Modern Europe* (Oxford: Oxford University Press, 1975).

8. This is extensivly described and analyzed in part B (especially B VI) of Schilling, *Internationale Beziehungen, 1559–1660* (above, note 1).

9. Werner Welzig, ed., *Erasmus von Rotterdam, Ausgewählte Schriften*, (Darmstadt: Wissenschaftliche Buchgesellschaft, 1968), 5:428.

10. Ibid., 5:411, 412.

11. Quotations from Holger Thomas Gräf, "Bündnissysteme der Neuzeit. Strukturelle Bedingungen der Außenpolitik bis zur europäischen Pentarchie," *Historicum* (1996–97): 22–26, here 23.

12. Matthias Pohlig, "Konfessionelle Deutungsmuster internationaler Konflikte um 1600—Kreuzzug, Antichrist, Tausendjähriges Reich," *Archiv für Reformationsgeschichte* 93 (2002): 278–316.

13. See, for example, Philip Marnix van St. Aldegonde, *Trouwe Vermaninge aende Christelijcke Gemeijneten van Brabant* (Leiden, 1598); idem., *Het Boeck der Psalmen Davids* (Middelburg, 1591), preface. For the *Wilhelmus-Hymn*, see Adrianus Cornelius den Besten, *Wilhelmus van Nassouwe: Het gedicht en zijn dichter*, dissertation (Leiden: Martinus Nijhoff, 1983). See also Schilling, "Konfessionalisierung und Formierung" (above, note 4), 605 ff.

14. Uwe Sibeth, "Gesandter einer aufständischen Macht. Die ersten Jahre der Mission von Dr. Pieter Cornelisz. Brederode im Reich (1602–1609)," *Zeitschrift für Historische Forschung* 30 (2003): 19–52.

15. Correspondence of the Dutch envoy Pieter Cornelisz. Brederode: Den Haag Algemeen Rijksachief, Lias Duitsland, 6016 I and II, 14.2.1604, and so forth. When the American president today speaks of the axis of evil, he is apparently referring to purely worldly concerns: terrorism, infringements of human rights, and a lack of democracy. But I wonder whether at least some parts of American society (which, as is well known, are deeply religious) infer from this vocabulary connotations that form part of the tradition of the eschatological-apocalyptic thinking of the past, described in the text. Thus the fight against terrorism would fit into the early modern tradition of wars of religion, and Islamic fundamentalism would be confronted by a secularized fundamentalist mentality.

16. Quotet in Anton Gindely, *Geschichte des Dreißigjährigen Krieges* (Leipzig: Frytag, 1882) part 1, p. 112.

17. Andreas Edel, "Auf dem Weg in den Krieg. Zur Vorgeschichte der Intervention Herzog Maximilians I. von Bayern in Österreich und Böhmen 1620," *Zeitschrift für Bayerische Landesgeschichte* 65 (2002): 157–253.

18. Often reproduced, for example, in Schilling, *Aufbruch und Krise*, note 18, part 1, 393, 395.

19. Reimar Hansen, "Heinrich Rantzau und das Problem des europäischen Friedens," in *Zwischenstaatliche Friedenswahrung in Mittelalter und Früher Neuzeit*, ed. Heinz Duchhardt (Köln: Böhlau, 1991), 91–110.

20. The events and turning points are treated in detail in my book *Konfessionalisierung und Staatsinteressen* (above, note 1). A recent excellent synthesis on the Thirty Years' War in English is Ronald G. Asch's *The Thirty Years' War: The Holy Roman Empire and Europe, 1618–48* (New York: St. Martin's Press, 1997).

21. The 450th anniversary of the Peace of Westphalia resulted in a reappraisal of the conditions, the structure, and the meaning of that peace. See esp. the three-volume catalogue of the exhibition *1648 — War and Peace* by the European Council, ed. by Klaus Bußmann and Heinz Schilling (Münster: Veranstaltungsgesellschaft, 1998).

22. See the definition in: Wilhelm Grewe, *Epochen der Völkerrechtsgeschichte* (Baden-Baden: Nomos, 1988), 339.

23. This is the first sentence of the Westfalian Peace Treaties. See Antje Oschmann, ed., *Die Friedensverträge mit Frankreich*

und Schweden, part 1, *Urkunden* (*Acta Pacis Westphalicae*. Serie III, Reihe B, Bd. 1), (Münster: Aschendorff, 1998).

24. Riv. Apol. Disc., OT IV, 701b; the quotation is from Posthumus Meyjes, *Irenicist*, 63.

25. Heinz Schilling, *Höfe und Allianzen. Deutsche Geschichte von 1648 bis 1763* (Berlin: Siedler, 1989); pbk., Siedler Deutsche Geschichte, vol. 5, 1998).

Index

Index

ment in, 56; popular pressures against migrants in, 45–46
Confessio Augustana, 19
confessionalization, 11–32; and acceleration of social change around 1600, 17–28; bringing Jews into paradigm of, 27–28; confessional fundamentalism, 68–69, 77, 78–84; explicit confessions in, 19–20; in general trend of European civilization, 18; and modernization, 14, 18–19, 26–27, 85; and nationalism, 20–21; and secularization, 28–30, 31, 83; and state formation, 10, 21, 23, 67–68, 72–77; total confrontation in, 68, 71, 77; widespread social influence of, 18–27. *See also* confessional migration; multiconfessionalism
confessional migration, 33–63; commercial factors in, 44–45, 54; concern over destabilization by, 46–48; cultural dynamism of, 55–60; defined, 38; dissenting migrants, 40; duration of, 38, 39; early migration from Habsburg territories, 41–49; as feature of Latin Europe, 10; as intermediate between medieval and later migration, 41; long-term economic and cultural consequences of, 52–63; migrants' reaction to segregation, 49–52; in modernization, 40–41; number of migrants, 38–39; peregrine experience of, 60–63; popular pressures against, 45–46; skills, expertise, and innovation disseminated by, 54; as source of dynamism, 37, 41; typology of, 35–49; varia-

tion in conditions of settlement for, 48–49; waves of, 37. *See also* Calvinist migrants; Dutch Protestant migrants; Sephardic Jews; Walloon Protestant migrants
Confessiones Helveticae, 19
conversos, 22
Court, Jan and Pieter de la, 99n.20
Cromwell, Oliver, 29
Crouzet, Denis, 18
Crusades, 16
"cuius regio eius religio" principle, 38, 47, 49
cultural relativism, rejection of, 5
"Cultural Reorientation and the Fundamental Principles of the Humanities" program, 91n.14

Danubian Principalities, 72
deists, 16, 28
Denmark, 72, 77, 79
Deutsche Christen, 63, 110n.57
diplomacy, 69
dove of peace, 31–32, 83
Düren, 57
Dutch Protestant migrants, 41–49; dissenting minority formed by, 40; long-term economic and cultural consequences of, 52–63; motives of, 44; number of, 38; popular pressures against, 45–46; in process of confessional migration, 37; reaction to segregation of, 49–52; social composition of, 43; underground churches of, 40
Dutch Republic: Calvinist migrants in, 48; economic consequences of Calvinist and Sephardic immigration, 54–55. *See also* Amsterdam

Index

migrants in, 45; Sephardic
Jews in, 44, 48
Frederick V of the Palatinate, 78
freethinkers, 16, 28
fundamentalism: confessional,
68–69, 77, 78–84; current
threat of, 68, 83; in French
Revolution, 86; as tendency in
European history, 68

Geistlicher Rauffhandel, 78
Gemünd valley, 57
Geneva, 76
Germany: Catholic-Calvinist
confrontation in, 76; concern over destabilizing effect
of migrants in, 47–48; confessional migrants in, 38, 39;
confession in internal power
struggle in, 73; "cuius regio
eius religio" principle in, 38,
47, 49; Deutsche Christen,
63, 110n.57; Dutch Protestant migrants in, 43, 47–48,
49; dynamism of confes-
sional migrants in, 55; economic consequences of
Dutch and Walloon immigration, 54, 55; Jewish influence
in, 98n.18; London stranger
churches hindered from entering, 60; Lutheran influence
in, 21; multiconfessionalism in, 22; Prussia, 70; Rhine
Palatinate, 71, 78; Sweden
influenced by, 23. *See also*
Aix-la-Chapelle; Cologne;
Frankfurt; Hamburg
Ghent, 43
global history, 6, 7
globalization: European historiography influenced by, 5–8; as
product of European expansion, 6–7

Goethe, Johann Wolfgang von, 49
Grotius, Hugo (Hugo de Groot),
80, 84
Gustavus Adolphus, King of Sweden, 24, 25

Habsburgs: in Catholic bloc of
states, 71; Long Turkish War,
72; migration from territories
of, 41–49; universalism of, 69.
See also Holy Roman Empire
Haemstede, Adrian van, 51–52
Hamburg: concern over destabilization by migrants in, 46,
47; Dutch Protestant migrants
in, 43, 45, 49; economic consequences of confessional
migrants in, 56; popular pressures against migrants in, 45,
105n.24; Sephardic Jews settle
in, 39, 43–45, 46
handel op de vijand, 55
Hanseatic League, 72
Hartlib, Samuel, 29
Henry IV, King of France, 24, 30
heretics, 22, 46
historiography: globalization's
influence on, 5–8; national
versus transnational, 3–4
Hobbes, Thomas, 80, 95n.6
Holy Roman Empire: and Brederode's Protestant alliance, 77;
Charles V, 22, 42, 70; internal
conflict in, 72; Lutheranism
legally protected in, 76; Thirty
Years' War in, 79. *See also*
Habsburgs
Huguenots: in Berlin, 39; historical prominence of, 41,
103n.15; number of, 39; in
process of confessional migration, 37; Saint Bartholomew's
Eve massacre, 71, 76
Humbert of Silva Candida, 15

Index

Hungary, 72
Hus, Jan, 17

Illuminati, 28
Inquisition, 20
interests of state, 70, 72, 86
Islam: confessionalization contrasted with groupings in, 85–86; influence in European religious life, 14; Ottoman Empire, 69, 72; Spanish self-assertion toward, 21
Italy, Protestant migrants from, 37, 38

Jansenism, 29
Jesuits, 26
Jews: bringing into paradigm of confessionalization, 27–28; Dutch tolerance of, 48; early modern European history from perspective of, 3; influence in European religious life, 14, 29, 98n.18; peregrine experience and tolerance of, 62; pogroms against, 16. See also Sephardic Jews
Johann III, King of Sweden, 23
Jonker, Ed, 91n.14

Kant, Immanuel, 31
Kaplan, Yosef, 53
Kirchenspaltung, 17–18
Kołakowski, Leszek, 28
Komensky (Comenius), Jan Amos, 29
Koselleck, Reinhard, 9
Krefeld, 57
Kühn, Johannes, 29

Landeskirchen, 62
Lasky, Jan (Johannes a Lasco), 60, 61
Latin Europe: capacity for per-petual change of, 13–14; Christian theology does not monopolize religion in, 14; church-state relationship in, 15–16; confessionalization and acceleration of social change around 1600, 17–28; dualism of sacred and secular in, 15–16; Greek Orthodox Europe distinguished from, 8–9, 14–15; key characteristics of, 9–10; religious differentiation in, 19–20; religious profile of, 13–32; tendency toward secularization in, 16, 31; unique dynamism of, 9. See also Austria; Belgium; England; France; Germany; Netherlands; Spain; Sweden; Switzerland
law: as key characteristic of Latin Europe, 9; in overcoming confessional fundamentalism, 80, 82
Leiden, 39
Leo IX, Pope, 15
limpieza de sangre, 16–17, 21, 22
Lithuania, Union of Brest and Orthodox of, 9
Livonia, 72
Lollards, 17
London: concern over destabilization by migrants in, 46; Dutch Protestant migrants settle in, 43, 45; economic consequences of confessional migrants in, 56; Sephardic Jews settle in, 39, 40, 43–45, 48; stranger churches of Lasky, 60
Louis XIV, King of France, 86
Lutheran Church: apocalypticism in politics of, 75; areas of influence of, 21; Book of Con-

Index

cord, 19; Calvinist migrant experience contrasted with, 62–63; *Confessio Augustana*, 19; confessional culture of, 20; "cuius regio eius religio" principle privileges, 49; in differentiation of European Christianity, 19; discipline of, 26; Flaccian Lutherans, 62, 110n.55; legal protection of, 76; Pietism in, 29; in Sweden, 22–25; visitations in, 20

man, pessimistic versus optimistic concepts of, 30
Marian Exiles, 39
Marnix, Philip, 76
Maximilian, Duke of Bavaria, 78
Mennonites, 57
Michael Kerullarios, 15
middle class (bourgeoisie): Calvinists migrants in rise of early modern, 57–60; Jesuit influence on, 26
migration: influence in Latin Europe, 10; pressure for integration of immigrants, 4–5; types of, 36. *See also* confessional migration
minorities, 33–63; dissenting, 40; influence in Latin Europe, 10. *See also* migration
modernity: Catholic antimodernism, 13, 27; confessionalization and modernization, 14, 18–19, 26–27; confessional migration in modernization, 40–41, 85; dark side of modernization, 16–17; dialectic of religious and secular in modernization, 30–31; Latin Europe's tendency toward, 16; and traditionalism as dialectically related, 53

Monschau, 57
morality: in confessional churches, 25–26; confessional migrants seek moral purity, 51, 52; official theology and, 29
multiconfessionalism: areas of influence of, 21, 22; in the Netherlands, 22, 48; as positive outcome of *Kirchenspaltung*, 18; renaissance after collapse of communism, 9
multiculturalism, crisis in concept of, 4–5

nationalism: confessionalization and, 20–21; rise of new, 4. *See also* state formation
National Science Organization (Netherlands), 4
Netherlands: and Brederode's Protestant alliance, 77; Catholic-Calvinist confrontation in, 76; conditions of settlement for migrants in, 48; early migration from Habsburg territories of, 41–49; Jewish influence in, 98n.18; multiconfessionalism in, 22, 48; national history as interest in, 5; nonconfessional denominations in, 28; optimistic concept of man develops in, 99n.20; in Protestant bloc of states, 71; re-Catholicization of southern, 43; sees itself as God's chosen people, 76; Spanish hegemony challenged by, 70, 72; Spanish military intervention in, 42. *See also* Amsterdam; Belgium; Dutch Protestant migrants; Dutch Republic; Walloon Protestant migrants

Index

Index

religio-vinculum-societatis
maxim, 18, 21, 47, 94n.6
Rhine Palatinate, 71, 78
Richelieu, Cardinal, 70, 74
Roman Catholic Church. *See*
Catholic Church
Roman law, 9, 80
Rubens, Peter Paul, 69
Rüsen, Jörn, 90n.13
Russia, 70, 72

Saint Bartholomew's Eve massacre, 71, 76
Salzburgian exiles, 37, 39
Sandys, Edwin, 94n.6
Scandinavia: Denmark, 72, 77,
79; early seventeenth-century
conflict in, 72; Lutheran influence in, 21; Lutheranism
legally protected in, 76. *See
also* Sweden
schepchen Godes, 61, 109n.52
Schism of 1054, 15
Schleiden valley, 57
secularization: in compromise
ending Thirty Years' War, 80–
84; confessionalization and,
28–30, 31, 83; gains upper
hand in late eighteenth century, 13; Latin Europe's tendency toward, 16, 31; new
stability of secular order of
autonomous states, 84–86
Sephardic Jews: in Amsterdam,
39, 43–45; business connections of, 44–45, 54; dogmatic
and moral purity sought by,
51, 52; economic elite among,
59–60; exclusive identity
developed by, 50; excommunication among, 51–52; favorite destinations of, 43–44;
Fettmilch rebellion against,
46, 48; in Frankfurt, 44, 48;
in Hamburg, 39, 43–45, 46;

in London, 39, 40, 43–45,
48; long-term economic and
cultural consequences of
migrants, 52–63; migrate from
Iberia, 22, 37, 41–49; popular
pressures against settlement
by, 45–46; reaction to segregation of, 49–52
Sidney, Sir Philip, 69
Sigismund III Vasa, King of Sweden, 23
1688 (Wills), 6
Socinians, 28
Spain: anti-French policy of, 74;
Brederode calls for Protestant
alliance against, 77; in Catholic bloc of states, 71; century
of hegemony of, 70, 72; international Catholicism split by,
74; military intervention in
Netherlands, 42; northwestern sea powers oppose, 72;
Reconquista, 16; Sephardic
migration from, 22, 37, 41–49;
Sephardic migration weakens,
54; Tridentine Catholicism in,
21–22
Spanish Armada, 71, 76
Spanish Fury, 76
Spinoza, Baruch de, 29, 52,
99n.20
Spiritualism, 28
state formation: birth of international state system, 65–86;
and confessionalization, 10,
21, 23, 67–68, 72–77; and crisis of early seventeenth century, 67, 70–77; new stability
of secular order of autonomous states, 84–86; as not
complete before 1650, 69;
periodization of early modern
state relations, 69–70; religion
and early modern state power,
67–70

123

Index

Stolberg, 57–59

Sweden: and Brederode's Protestant alliance, 77; Charles IX, 23, 24; Dutch Protestant migrants settle in, 43, 48; in early seventeenth-century conflict in Baltic-Scandinavian region, 72; economic consequences of Dutch and Walloon immigration, 54; German influence on, 23; Gustavus Adolphus, 24, 25; Lutheran confessional identity in, 22–25; Polish Wasa's rule in, 23–24; in Thirty Years' War, 24, 79; Westphalian Peace system guaranteed by, 70

Switzerland: Calvinist/Reformed influence in, 21; Dutch Protestant migrants settle in, 43; Geneva, 76; multiconfessionalism in, 22

39 Articles, 19

Thirty Years' War, 79; alliance and cabinet wars contrasted with, 86; compromise in ending of, 79–84; Peace of Westphalia, 31–32, 68, 70, 79, 81, 82, 83; Sweden wages as battle for Reformation, 24

towns: dogmatic and moral purity sought in, 46, 105n.26; migrants' influence in, 35, 36. *See also* Aix-la-Chapelle; Amsterdam; Antwerp; Cologne; Frankfurt; Hamburg; London

traditionalism, 53, 55

Transylvania, 72

Treaty of Oliva, 68, 79

Tridentine Catholic Church: areas of influence of, 21; and Catholic bloc of states, 71;

confessional culture of, 20; in differentiation of European Christianity, 19; discipline of, 26; *Professio fidei Tridentina*, 19; in Spain, 21–22; visitations in, 20

Turks, 69, 72

Ukraine, multiconfessional renaissance after collapse of communism in, 9

underground churches, 40

Union of Brest, 9

Vaudoise, 37, 38

Vichttal, 57

visitations, 20

Walloon Protestant migrants, 41–49; dissenting minority formed by, 40; in Leiden, 39; long-term economic and cultural consequences of, 52–63; motives of, 44; number of, 38; popular pressures against, 45–46; in process of confessional migration, 37; reaction to segregation of, 49–52; social composition of, 43; underground churches of, 40

Weber, Max, 16, 57

Wee, Herman van der, 6, 7

Wehler, Hans-Ulrich, 89n.8, 90n.12

Wesel, 39, 44

West-Ost-Gefälle, 8

Wilhelm, Landgrave of Hessen, 74

"Wilhelmus-hymn," 76

William of Orange, 76

Wills, John, 6, 7

world civilizations, comparison of types of, 7–8

Wyclif, John, 17